Table Settings, Entertaining, and Etiquette

BY THE SAME AUTHOR:

Technical Floristry
Flower Craft
The Book of Table Arrangements
Party Decorations for Christmas and Other Occasions
How to Make Flower Decorations
Simplified Flower Arrangements
Flower Arrangements through the Year

Table Settings, Entertaining, and Etiquette

A HISTORY AND GUIDE

Patricia Easterbrook Roberts

A Studio Book

THE VIKING PRESS

NEW YORK

To Ann Valentine Cesare

Text Copyright © 1967 by Patricia Easterbrook Roberts
All rights reserved

First published in 1967 by The Viking Press, Inc.
625 Madison Avenue, New York, N. Y. 10022

Published simultaneously in Canada by
The Macmillan Company of Canada Limited

Third printing December 1968

Library of Congress catalog card number: 67-25918
Text and black-and-white plates printed in U.S.A.
Color plates printed in Italy

Contents

Introduction

Amistress of a house once wrote, "The direction of a table is no inconsiderable branch of a lady's concern, as it involves judgment in expenditure; respectability of appearance; and the comfort of her husband and those who partake their hospitality."

Every woman has her own audience, and her own challenge to meet. This is a daily job. Sometimes, however, she feels a lack of appreciation, and in consequence her best efforts in this direction are put forward only for special occasions — and for special guests. And yet, the most important people in our lives are those with whom we share the dining table most often. They are the ones we should always try to please.

Along with cooking, the arrangement of the table and the serving of food can be an outlet for the creative woman, and if she is interested in making an art of it, her pleasure in daily living can be doubled. The table is, or should be, the warm center of the home.

I became interested in gathering together this material not only because I enjoy history but because I feel that much can be learned from the way people in every part of the world decorate their tables, and cook and serve food. In addition to aesthetics, there is also the practical side, and this book is intended as a guide to setting the table for both every day and special occasions.

In the planning of a setting, it is often the house and the room itself that dictate the theme. To some extent this should always be so. After this there is the question of the materials that are on hand — sometimes an interesting collection of fine china, pewter, or pottery, suggesting a special kind of arrangement. And last, the particular character and activities of the household have a very special influence on what we do.

In giving my lectures I soon discovered how fascinated people were with what I was able to tell them about the use of dishes and the different placement of silverware and glasses in other countries. This leads directly to the question of customs and, in turn, to history, which includes the story of the first tools man used and how these gradually developed into the tableware we know today. The more my researches continued, the more interesting the whole subject became, and I delved for further information in museums and libraries, both here and abroad, that would link our modern customs with the past.

I hope that the reader will find useful information and entertaining pictures that encourage him not only to enjoy the formality of traditional settings and the antiques of our forebears, but also to find stimulation in creating an original and colorful table setting.

OPPOSITE: Banquet of Heracles and Eurytion. Detail from a Corinthian crater c. 600 B.C.

Wall painting from the tomb of Rekhmire in Thebes, c. 1450 B.C.

8

ce sauut qi pranre sor ses espaulles .a par   et mon lesancel le roi presqueor et li ont

King Arthur and the Knights of the Round Table at their Christmas feast, depicted in a fourteenth-century French manuscript.
Merlin the magician is welcoming Sir Galahad, who will sit in the
chair which is left between King Arthur and Sir Lancelot.

10

1.

A Short History

his pictorial history really begins with the Renaissance. While a few documents exist from the early Greeks and Egyptians, and many Renaissance paintings depict religious scenes showing more-or-less imaginary settings, little material is available to us before the fourteenth century. From that time on, through the nineteenth century when photography was new, until now, we see countless examples of the habits and customs of setting the table and eating in many lands.

The majority of the paintings and prints depict polite society and the genteel accomplishments of each period. Even when Queen Elizabeth I had a picnic during the hunting season, it was managed with great style and awareness of court etiquette.

Of course, painters and engravers, like other artists, were governed by their own whims and foibles and allowances must therefore be made for artistic license in some of the paintings. However, since photographs of early times are not available, we must form our opinions on earlier periods through studying their literature and art.

The preparation and management of food, its presentation, and the comfort and ease of those participating are just as important at a picnic or a banquet today as they were in the past. Today flatware, china, and other table accessories are universally available in a range wide enough to satisfy anyone's taste, but in the sixteenth century only court functions in a royal household could produce all that was needed for a really beautiful table display. In earlier pictures it is interesting to note the primitive design of the trestle tables (removed after the meal was finished), the heavy-looking trenchers, the occasional knife, the use of the hands (which, as the saying goes, "were made before knives and forks"), and the varying lengths of the table covers.

In the Renaissance period, and on into the sixteenth century, we see the stool replaced with chairs, and the appearance of comports, covered dishes, and other serving vessels, which made table settings more interesting.

Medieval paintings show the seating arranged on one side of the table; this was partly for political reasons, at a time when the assassination of kings and princes was relatively common and seating against the wall eliminated the possibility of an enemy's approaching from the rear. Also, entertainments were common during or after the meal and with this plan the host and his guests were conveniently placed.

In the seventeenth and eighteenth centuries we begin to see a more friendly pattern in both general seating and individual place service. For special occasions separate tables were set apart for royalty or other guests of honor, and the side tables displayed a greater variety of dishes and food. Ornate candelabra added light and glitter to banquet tables.

Napery became increasingly important, and sometimes we see the cloth draped for

Detail from "The Story of Griselda" (a series of paintings by an unknown Italian artist, c. 1500), depicts the banquet for Griselda, who was restored to her husband and children. A

very special effects. Several pictures show large serviettes, or napkins, either in use over the knees or thrown casually on the table, and sometimes for a more practical, if not aesthetic, reason, even tied around the neck.

Wine coolers on the floor nearby and glasses or goblets being filled or held ready for a toast improve the action of the pictures and help to give the general mood of the period: that of gay abandonment to the joy of good company and good dining.

Although we know that tools other than the knife were used on the table they appear infrequently in the earlier pictures. These tools were kept in traveling sets in shagreen cases, and were probably closely held on to by the guests until they actually needed to use them. It was harder then to replace a missing knife or fork than it is today.

fringed cloth covers the table board, which is supported by trestles. It was the custom to move the board and trestles after the meal. The serving men are carrying scarflike napkins.

RIGHT: The Princely Banquet. A German woodcut made in 1491 shows the Prince at a separate table.

LEFT: A Flemish family at table, in the fifteenth century. The high chairs allow for the ladies' voluminous skirts.

LEFT: A German woodcut shows diners entertained by musicians in a minstrel gallery of the early sixteenth century.

OPPOSITE: This miniature from the early-fifteenth-century prayer book *Les Très Riches Heures* shows the Duc de Berry dining in his castle. On the trestle table is a sumptuous boat-shaped vessel called a nef, for holding dishes. In those days everyone ate with his fingers.

OPPOSITE: At an early-sixteenth-century Flemish feast, a lord and lady are entertained by torch dancers, a jester, and musicians. They dine by candlelight at their cloth-covered table beneath a canopy.

RIGHT: An engraving (c. 1575) shows Queen Elizabeth seated on a high stool at a picnic during a royal hunt. Her subjects had to sit on the ground, but were at least allowed to eat from a cloth.

"A Nobleman at His Table." The vessels and dishes on the table show the skill of the sixteenth-century Italian craftsman and the wealth of the owner. The silver nef on the right of the table was probably used, in this instance, for displaying costly spices.

19

LEFT: Behind the scenes in an Elizabethan manor a large staff prepares a meal for the evening.

BELOW: An allegorical painting by the sixteenth-century Flemish artist Pieter Pourbus shows graybeard (Sapiens) with the lady (Fidutia) who represents loyalty. The presence of the Three Graces and Cupid suggests that love and folly are only for youth.

ABOVE: On November 18, 1623, King James I of England and his son Charles entertained Spanish ambassadors. The use of a square table with seating on two sides, laden with platters of food, is typical of the period.

ABOVE: In 1633 King Louis XIII held a banquet at Fontainebleau in honor of newly created knights. The heavily laden tables are covered with cloths which show the mark of the linen press.

RIGHT: The shapes of banquet tables (with seating on both sides), high-backed chairs, individual candlesticks, and elaborate decorative pieces as well as food platters are shown here in a German print, 1717. This is the Cardinal's Residence in Regensburg.

BELOW: Candelabra, chandeliers, and crystal goblets bring sparkle and elegance to the dining tables set in the Salle des Festins at Versailles in 1763. The occasion was the celebration of the Treaty of Paris.

OPPOSITE: "The Ham Feast," painted in 1735 by Nicolas Lancret, illustrates the French enjoyment of wine. Bottles and wine coolers are shown in the foreground and a pair of porcelain *cachepots* are set on the table. It is interesting to see that a spoon is provided — and that the napkins are giant size.

In the nineteenth century elegant dining reached its height. The amount and variety of food served, and consumed, in the average well-to-do household quite staggers our diet-conscious minds today. Large homes and a plentiful supply of servants made lengthy dinners and endless service the pattern for a socially successful evening. In the 1890s public

ABOVE: "The Thatched House Club," painted by Thomas Sheperd, shows the Englishman's predilection for men's clubs. Typical of the nineteenth century is the architectural confection decoration displayed in the center of the table. OPPOSITE: "The Dinner Party," by Henry Sargent, is the American counterpart. The table is without a cover for the fruit-and-nut course and the accompanying wine.

dining began to rival private dining, and the French restaurant or its imitation became the most fashionable in London, New York, and every other large international city. Certain British customs also had a strong influence in America. Teatime, an English innovation, rapidly became popular and, surprisingly enough, Americans were soon consuming more tea than the English.

BELOW: A banquet given by the Corporation of London on November 9, 1837, for Queen Victoria, in the Guildhall, where the Lord Mayor's banquets are still held. The cloth for the royal table is very decorative, the seating plan is formal, and the tables are laid out in a symmetrical pattern.

BELOW: "Christmas in the South," a nineteenth-century illustration, depicts people of all ages at an informal egg-nog party.

"A Pic-nick, Camden, Maine," painted by Jerome B. Thompson. The informality associated with picnicking and the enjoyment of the outdoors seem to make all food taste better.

Great social changes had started in the nineteenth century, owing to the industrial revolution, and after World War I these were particularly felt when servants began to find jobs with better hours and pay in factories. This trend continued, and through the depression years the lady of the house began to do many, if not all, of the chores herself. Other changes were brought about by the needs of the twentieth-century businessman. Lunchtime became shorter and the fare lighter. Stricter office hours also tended to cut down the time allowed for breakfast, for the head of the household rushed to arrive at work on time.

27

The dining room itself was once a great hall, then it became a very elegant room, and finally, in the houses that have been built in the last several decades, it has tended to dwindle to a small area adjacent to the living room, even in well-to-do households. In apartments this is particularly true, if indeed the dining room is not a mere extension of the kitchen. But, wherever they can afford it, people today are reverting to the enjoyment, convenience, and importance of a more gracious meal set in a separate room especially designed for the purpose.

The great problem of service has been overcome either with organized outside professional help or with inside modern equipment and carefully organized planning. The servants of today are such innovations as dishwashers and kitchens designed to save as many steps as possible. Other obvious economies in time and trouble relate to the service itself. For instance, in the nineteenth century two tablecloths were used, one being removed after the main course. Today, although table covers of one kind or another are essential for formal occasions, in many elegant homes precious china is set directly on old wood. Fine mats and scarves are also used to create imaginative settings and cut down on the maintenance problem. Recently, in England, traditional lace tablecloths in Victorian patterns reappeared on the market for use with old china and silver, which so many families have inherited from the last century.

Treasured eighteenth-century heirlooms that have survived the vicissitudes of the past still grace fine tables today, and are greatly in demand. Old Canton, once common Chinese Export Porcelain brought into Europe and America as ballast on ships, is now sought by collectors and is probably responsible for the popularity of the blue-and-white china patterns now designed by modern factories.

Spode's Tower pattern, originally derived from a 1795 engraving and now altered to fit the Gadroon shape, is once more quite generally available. So is English cutlery in traditional designs. This does not mean that modern simpler designs are not popular — it is just that there is a natural demand for all kinds of good design, no matter in what century they originated.

Certainly, appreciation for the quality of the craftsmanship of centuries gone by is on the increase. Great-grandmother's things, once considered old-fashioned and obsolete, have returned to use when the setting is right for them. I doubt that there is any leading decorator who does not advocate the blending of well-designed and well-made furniture and accessories of different centuries, provided this is done with knowledge and understanding.

The hours for eating and the names of the meals have changed often enough to confuse us slightly when we read about the past. Also, the traveler abroad sometimes has a hard time adapting his eating habits to those of the country he is visiting. In England, for instance, tea is a traditional meal; in America it is not, and consequently dinnertime is usually later in England than it is in the United States and Canada. Later dinners are common on the Continent, and also in Latin America, where larger lunches (and siestas in the

"Christmas at Home," painted in New York State by Grandma Moses, the well-known primitive artist. One table is set for the adults, and one for the children.

afternoon) are customary. Part of the fun of traveling is adapting oneself to each new situation and participating in the local customs and festive ceremonies that have been handed down from earlier generations.

Through reading and travel our knowledge of other nations and customs has broadened so that we have a much better understanding of what to expect and what not to expect, and therefore how best to please our host — an ancient and still prevailing custom.

The visitor, when journeying the length and breadth of the United States, never knows when he may enter a "patch" of Europe, Asia, or some other transplanted culture. He simply puts his napkin across one knee, spreads it widely, tucks it under his chin, or ties it around his neck, and follows the manner of the host, the theme of the restaurant, and the custom of the community, and enjoys life with his fellow man.

An elegant table showing eighteenth-century Dresden porcelain of museum quality. The flowers in the center of the table were chosen to complement the colors in the porcelain. Vermeil cutlery and glasses of Bohemian crystal are set out on the cloth of white Flanders damask.

Meissen ornament.

2.
Entertaining around the World

Just as people have never traveled so extensively as they do today, they have never had the opportunity of enjoying shopping more. In no other century has such a variety of wares been more generally available. Intelligent shopping can produce fascinating and often unique treasures that provide material for unusual table settings: covers and napkins in exciting colors and materials; glass and earthenware that is primitive in its simplicity and practical to use; glittering crystal and china that echo the elegance of the past; and unusual centerpieces that lend themselves to many kinds of tables.

Whether you hanker for the food that goes with some of the exotic bowls and dishes of foreign origin that you have been tempted to purchase is immaterial. However, if you do — and can'obtain the ingredients — your setting and food can make for an evening that will be that much more original and entertaining. Many of the pictures in this chapter were taken on my travels or were sent to me by friends living abroad. The majority, however,

ABOVE: A Japanese setting shows covered bowls for soup, covered lacquered bowls for vegetables, scalloped dishes for fish, and plates for rice.

LEFT: A display of texture and design to please the eye of a Chinese guest.

OPPOSITE: The colors of the Japanese Imari plates (c. 1860) are cobalt and orange. The hand-wrought iron nasturtium candelabrum, branches of bittersweet on the table, and the napkins are in complementary shades of orange.

though international in appearance, were taken within twenty miles of my own home. These table settings have used family heirlooms and treasures old and new collected from distant countries; many of them were arranged in honor of foreign guests.

There is hardly a sophisticated household today that is not related in some way to another country, that does not at some time entertain a person who lives halfway or more across the world.

Whether a guest from afar is to come for a meal or for the night there are a few simple ways that we can be helpful to him. To begin with, the invitation — whether by telephone or by letter — should be explicit. The hour for eating should be understood (in different parts of the world, dinner can mean anything from six-thirty to ten o'clock). The kind of food planned might be hinted at, if not clearly explained, so that if your guest has some personal reason why he cannot eat it — or some special preferences (perhaps he is a vegetarian) — he can let you know in advance. There is nothing more embarrassing, for instance, than to serve meat on a day when certain religions forbid it.

Many Europeans prefer wine served with the meal, rather than cocktails or other spirits beforehand. Americans are used to ice water on the table, Europeans are not. Relatively few Europeans drink milk with their meals, while many Americans do. This is not to say that a foreigner will not usually want, and enjoy, a menu typical of the country he is visiting, but the good host tries to plan for every contingency. One thoughtful gesture is to have fruit juices or sodas on hand for those who do not take hard liquor or wine.

A guest newly arrived from abroad should be called for rather than be made to venture for miles in a new country in which transportation may be confusing to him. If this is not possible, written instructions that can be studied and understood ahead of time, including your telephone number and a little map, if this will help, are considerations that should enable your guest to arrive on time in a happy frame of mind. Your guest may know no one in the country besides yourself, or else he may have a letter of introduction from a mutual friend, so that even you are a stranger to him. In either case he will find a small party less confusing than a large one. Most foreigners who visit are likely to have at least some understanding of English. However, if you can invite friends who have some knowledge of his language, this cannot help making things easier for him. And, of course, someone in the same profession, or who shares artistic, literary, or political interests, or who has a knowledge of his country, will help the conversation to flow more easily too.

OPPOSITE: An elegant luncheon table with a flowers-and-birds theme. The delicate Flora Danica pattern, originally designed for Catherine the Great, and made by the Royal Copenhagen Porcelain Company, reproduces a collection of wild flowers. The cloth is fine pale pink lawn appliquéd with geranium flowers, the glasses are Lalique, and the flatware is English sterling.

OPPOSITE: The story of the petticoat government of China from A.D. 655 to 704, under the famous Empress Wu, may not be the happiest topic for mealtime conversation; however, the Empress became a paragon of virtue before she died at the age of eighty. This colorful scroll portrait of her is a handsome feature of this room, and looks well with the terra-cotta pot, flowering amaryllis, old Chinese tea caddy, bread dish, and covered lacquered tea bowl. The Chinese table is inlaid with mother-of-pearl.

LEFT: The Saun Pakkad Palace, Bangkok. The palace consists of a group of Thai houses, one of which is seen here. ABOVE: A table set in one of the private gardens. The centerpiece is made from twisted seaplants, with fresh flower heads inserted for extra color.

When entertaining people from other lands, it is a good idea to include members of differing age groups. Foreign guests often get along with children of all ages extremely well. It is easy to understand and respond to a child's uncomplicated curiosity.

Obviously the more warmth and hospitality the host displays, and the greater care he takes in planning a friendly evening, the greater service he is doing, not only for himself but for his country, in breaking down some of the delicate barriers that separate one nation from another.

A beautiful lace cloth in the Spanish tradition was used for a table decorated with grapes and a garland of vines — a motif repeated in a gold border etched on the crystal goblets. A pair of sculptured bronze pheasants gives height to the decoration.

Classical Greek motifs appear in the gold design on the service plates, the three pottery vases, and the chairs and legs of the table. Two of the vases, painted in terra cotta and black, make handsome candle holders, and the other holds grape leaves and white poppies. The small silver goblets are for ouzo. The marble head of a girl is two thousand years old.

RIGHT: A table set in Italy for a Christmas Eve dinner shows Richard-Ginori fine porcelain china. In Italy there is no particular rule for the napkin placement.

BELOW: This dining room, in an English Tudor home, has seen many changes in eating habits. Glasses are set for the traditional three wines—sherry, champagne, and port. Contemporary English place settings are wider than American simply because all the cutlery is laid out initially and a bread-and-butter plate is used for formal dinners.

ABOVE: A place setting from Sweden that shows the clean, graceful lines her designers have made famous.

LEFT: A picnic near an old water mill on the shores of Lake Geneva looks inviting with the vineyard baskets, a bunch of wild flowers, a Tyrolean hat, and an indispensable walking stick.

OPPOSITE: Vineyards make a fitting background for a fondue luncheon. The bread drawer in the old Swiss table may still be used for bread, but it also makes a convenient place to store table silver. The white flowers and grasses were gathered from the roadside, and the green hellebore was picked in a nearby garden.

OPPOSITE: In the dining room of this English house Jacobean paneling creates a warm background for pewter and copper. Pewter service plates, under copper gratin dishes, look as appropriate in a modern setting as they do here. ABOVE: The house, with its sixteenth-century timbers.

3.
Houses
and Tables

This chapter shows the room and table setting in relation to the architecture of the house. Although examples have been taken from England, the Continent, and the Orient, most are from the United States, which is so international that within its boundaries, and in Canada, too, are houses that architecturally reflect the styles of many lands. Some, indeed, have been transported brick by brick from Europe; others have been copied exactly or in part, and others are indigenous to the extent that they follow the traditional styles evolved by the early settlers.

The East Coast of the United States abounds in elegant and dignified Georgian manors based on English prototypes, solid old stone farmhouses built by the Pennsylvania Germans, stately square houses of the Federalist period, New England salt boxes, and the Cape Cod houses that stretched and grew with the family. As the virgin timberlands

This house in Connecticut was built by Gideon Lounsbury, c. 1780. OPPOSITE: In the dining room, the fireplace provided heat and a place for cooking. The pewter ale jug, drinking vessels, and the plates, c. 1750, are much sought after by collectors today. The cake, cooked in the mold on the hearth, was made from an eighteenth-century recipe.

opened up in the Middle West, great Victorian houses of wood, based on English designs and covered with gingerbread ornamentation, settled their huge comfortable quarters on Main Street. In contrast, the lacy ironwork on the beautiful Southern homes stands as graceful testimony to the cultured English and French immigrants who settled there.

The West came under the Spanish influence at first, for its climate encouraged the enjoyment of patios and walled gardens. Soon, however, individualists wanted homes that seemed to grow out of the land itself; they wanted the materials around them used in construction, with wide windows, and areas where the house and the outdoors could be enjoyed as one. Here, the influence of the Orient, particularly Japan, is also to be seen. This type of architecture is perhaps most suited to the climate of America's West Coast.

The international pattern of living has spread to all corners of the world. Therefore, with but slight differences, any of the ideas illustrated on these pages are applicable, from the design point of view, to any civilized region.

44

ABOVE: An engraving of the White House, Washington, dated 1850, shows the north side, which has been faithfully preserved although changes have constantly been made to the interior. BELOW: Place setting in the White House.

OPPOSITE: This unique table of in-laid marble, which seats thirty people, was made in Florence, and is set with priceless china, vermeil, and Venetian glass.

Woodlawn Plantation, in
Mount Vernon, Virginia, was
begun in 1802 under the direction of General Washington
as a home for Lawrence and
Nelly Custis Lewis. OPPOSITE:
The dining room. In the style
of 1812, the table was first
covered with two cloths. After
the meat and fish courses were
removed an elaborate dessert
course was set up on the lower
cloth. Then fruit and wine
were served on the bare table.

RIGHT: The rear portico of the Wickham-Valentine House, Richmond, Virginia, now known as the Valentine Museum.

A dining room in a house featuring seventeenth- and eighteenth-century furnishings. The Bolognese oak table has three drawers on either side for storage of silver and linen. Eighteenth-century early Capo di Monte plates, each with a different family crest, go well with Venetian glasses of the same period. The flatware, custom-made in the 1800s, is also Italian.

RIGHT: Porcelain ice-cream jar in three sections, the top and bottom for ice and the middle for ice cream. Thomas Jefferson brought the recipe for ice cream to the United States from France. BELOW: The dining room at the Wickham-Valentine House with a table setting for dessert course in the style of the 1840s. The pair of ice-cream jars is used.

Many people who have visited Japan have fallen under its spell and have not only brought home many souvenirs but have changed their homes or built modern ones in the Japanese tradition, such as the one above. However, Japanese works of art, furnishings, and accessories are so readily available in the West that a setting such as the one at right can be created locally. An adventurous hostess may also be inspired to produce Oriental menus and flower arrangements. The striped garden grasses over the buffet at left are inserted in lengths of bamboo which was purchased from a carpet store. The bamboo is fixed to a brass tray with florists' clay.

"Fruits of Autumn." Still life by James Peale.

4.
Why Set a Pretty Table?

"The table is the point for family reunion twice or three times a day, and nothing should be lacking that we can do to make those meetings pleasant and cheerful. No decoration will suffice to cover untidy napery, dim glass, or only partly cleaned silver. All details must be looked to, and then a perfect whole may be expected." This advice, taken from an English penny weekly dated 1896, has lost none of its validity.

Tables are set every day, by most housewives, for many kinds of meals of varying degrees of importance, from breakfast to theater suppers. Today some people think that setting an attractive table is an unnecessary fuss and bother, and they have time only for the bare necessities. Meals become just a daily chore to be handled with dispatch; the sooner they are over, the better. Unfortunately there are times when one has to eat a sandwich, and run. Eating "on the run" is perhaps better than not eating at all, but it is not complimentary to the food, the cook, or the setting — to say nothing about its effect on the digestive system. Everyone will agree that meals eaten in a pleasant and relaxed atmosphere are better for us, as well as being more enjoyable. It is our responsibility to create a pretty table, so that the meals are enjoyed in a setting that tempts one to linger over them and relax.

Snack bars and dinettes are convenient, of course, but the very casual quality of everything that goes with this type of setting produces a casual manner that too easily slips to no manners at all. I believe that every effort to set a pretty table is necessary in order to please oneself, to use one's creative abilities to the full, and, in consequence, to brighten the day and delight one's family and friends as best one can. Not only does this enhance the presentation of food and add zest to dining, but it also creates a feeling of unity (which seems

Italian Majolica with its beautiful colors and delightful designs makes a pretty table. Four dishes for cheeses and crackers and a central one holding nuts are decorated with charming bushy-tailed squirrels. Place settings are on one side of the table to enable the guests to enjoy a view of the garden.

to be better accomplished around the dining-room table than at any other place in the home) and sets a standard for the younger members of the household to follow.

A table should be well balanced. A pretty table also depends upon everything's being in proper proportion. A large table can look silly with a lot of small pieces dotted around. If your service requires many small extra dishes, keep them grouped on a suitable serving tray. In your centerpiece, too, color and flower forms should be grouped to create the "weight" that is necessary. In this respect, remember that some colors and textures appear heavier than others. For instance, warm colors like red and yellow are strong, advancing colors, while blue and white are cool, receding colors.

Napkins must be folded with care and placed properly so that the general effect is one of tidiness. It is always imperative to have impeccable napery, whether you use a cloth or mats or runners. If plastic is substituted for linen, as it might well be for breakfast and casual meals (but never for formal ones), it must be checked before every meal for cleanliness. Cleanliness is closely allied to beauty; a pretty table, like a pretty face, depends on soap and water. This machine age saves us much effort but we still have the final responsibility of seeing that our linen is spotless and that the china, glassware, and silver sparkle.

A table placed near a window, where a colorful garden or other charming view can be seen, is, of course, very pleasant. However, the art of interior decorating offers so much that no matter what the setting is, no dining room need be drab and unattractive. It is a great blessing today that we are no longer bound by rigid notions of what is proper in the way of furnishing or color schemes. Within the limits of good taste you can do exactly as you like and make the most of even the most unpromising situations. Although I do believe that for formal table settings it is best to keep more or less to one period, with experience it is possible, and often exciting, to combine periods in such ways that the new will complement the older pieces.

Setting a pretty dinner table is one of the most rewarding activities in the daily round of family life. The table is the "theater," or at least the "stage," for a nightly performance that can be as entertaining as any show on Broadway or London's West End. We should be just as eager to entertain the members of our family as we are to entertain any honored guest. Sincere compliments should flow from one to the other, for gratitude is the key to many a happy hour where warm words heal, just as much as good food. This important time of coming together for refreshment surely is the greatest opportunity to add beauty, laughter, consideration, and relaxation to our day so that everyone feels better for this experience.

OPPOSITE: In the top illustration a Spode feldspar porcelain tea set (c. 1800) is arranged on a Pembroke table (c. 1790) in front of the settee, and a pair of Wedgwood and Waterford candleholders (c. 1800) grace the tambour table. The lower photograph shows a simple, quick arrangement of carnations and tiny waxlike flowers. The nosegays are held together with rubber bands placed in glasses of various heights. String smilax introduces a touch of delicate green. The table was set in Sydney, Australia, where the wonderful long-lasting Geraldton wax flower is plentiful.

The King of Portugal entertains John of Gaunt. Fourteenth century.

5.
Table Linen

The term "table linen" is applied to any fabric or material used for a cloth or place mats for the dining table, and to the accompanying napkins. While china, flatware, and glass are bought and correlated with the idea that they will be used for many years and perhaps, with nominal care, will last a lifetime and more, linen is one of the elements of the table that allows for the greatest number of changes. In china, flatware, and glass, the best advice anyone can give you is "buy the finest you can afford"; linen can be extremely expensive, but it need not be — there is less convention nowadays and more ingenuity, imagination, and personal taste.

Linen provides the textured background for all the other elements; although they have texture too, we are more conscious of it in linen. Color is another quality that table linen contributes to the setting. The color on your table can express to the fullest your own enjoyment of the stimulating effect it can have in the room itself and as a complement to your china. It can be a contrast: if the plate is undecorated except for a gold or platinum border, the cloth might have an over-all pattern in any gay color or design; if the china has a soft aqua border, the cloth might be dove gray. If the predominant color on the china is perfect in your setting you can remain in that color range by having the cloth a lighter shade and napkins darker or vice versa (see pages 145 and 253). This monochromatic effect can enhance the appearance of the china. Plates decorated with delicate floral patterns and green leaves are always cool and charming on a cloth in any one of the myriad green shades available in regular table linen or yard goods. Dark tablecloths with matching napkins have become increasingly popular as a foil for the china, flatware, and glass. However, it is important to keep to the same tone so that the cloth is a background and does not overpower and kill the design and color on the dinnerware. Some of us can remember when all tablecloths were white and damask reigned supreme, and although both white as a color and damask as a material went out of fashion for everyday use, good damask has outlasted this period and is being used again in many households. White, although long replaced by off-white and cream for formal tables, is coming back into fashion in Irish and Belgian linens.

The degree of formality normally required in your entertaining will indicate the group of fabrics you are most likely to consider purchasing. Formal dinners and parties for special occasions call for imported lace, fine Madeira, appliquéd organdy, and the beautiful, hand-embroidered Marghab linen. For tables of unusual size or shape, pure silk yard goods may be made into handsome covers that launder beautifully. Most of these fine covers need a silence cloth or fitted pad underneath them to silence the placing of accessories and to anchor the cloth. All of them are also suitable for the tea table. Formality does not necessarily mean that one must be hedged in by convention. For instance, I have seen an extremely formal table setting with a cloth of Chinese brocade threaded with gold; and other unusual coverings, if beautifully made, can be equally pleasing.

Informal china and earthenware look best on hand-woven textiles, on linen in various weights, on rayon, or on any textured cloth that is in harmony with the tableware to be used. On the market today there are modern tablecloths in gay stripes, checks, floral patterns, and a remnant counter is a rich source of supply for those who want something different and like many changes.

The shape of the tablecloth should, of necessity, conform to the shape of the dining table, whether it is square, oblong, round, or oval. The oblong or rectangular table has been the most popular for many years, but there is a modern trend toward round tables that open up to an oval shape for extra seating. When measuring the table for a cloth, an overhang of from ten to fifteen inches on all sides must be allowed for. On a large banquet table, for a really luxurious effect, the cloth should hang over as far as conveniently possible.

Table mats have proved such a blessing in every way that it is hard to imagine how any household ever managed without them. These must, of course, be large enough to hold the entire place setting without being crowded, and never at any time should one mat overlap another. The edge of a mat should be even with the edge of the table; special shapes with one edge longer and slightly curved make this possible even on a round table. Tricky shapes and overhanging round mats are usually more trouble than they are worth and generally detract from the neatness of the setting. Nowadays mats are acceptable for all occasions except formal social functions, and for the tea table. They are made in a wide variety of materials, from the easy-to-care-for plastics (some of which look like fragile Venetian lace) to the most exquisite organdy and Thai silk. Handwoven fiber mats (from the Abaca plant) come from the Philippines. Woven straw mats come from Italy, Mexico, India, Hawaii, Haiti, Jamaica, and Japan. Those that are crudely woven are delightful when used with ironstone and other heavier earthenware in the proper setting. Table mats in place of tablecloths may save one from the tyranny of the ironing board, but they do expose the table top, which may therefore need a little extra cleaning and polishing. However, this can be a rewarding job, for the wood itself, when continually well polished, takes on a luster that contributes enormously to the attractiveness of the table setting.

A table runner, once part of a set with mats and napkins, is now popular, placed across the table to accommodate two settings. These runners or scarves may all be in the same color, or they may combine harmonious colors, stripes, or floral patterns. In fact, if made up out of yard goods, runners can be in any fabric, color, or pattern that ties in with the setting, tableware, and theme. Runners are less trouble to care for than a full tablecloth and a little more decorative than mats.

It is disappointing to buy a tablecloth that is charming, only to find that it spends most of its life in a linen drawer because the napkins are unsuitable — either too small or so fancy that laundering is a problem, or so thin that they cannot survive repeated laundering. When a matching set is purchased, usually for formal dinner parties, the napkins should be given careful consideration. The most important feature in a dinner napkin is its size, which certainly should not be less than 18 inches square if you want to be popular with your male guests, and for formal social functions, 24 inches square, hand hemmed, and matching the cloth. For a short while, oblong or rectangular napkins were made and called "lapkins" in America. This shape was thought to stay more easily on the lap.

A convenient-sized napkin for luncheon service is 15 inches square, and a soft, smooth, absorbent texture is naturally best. The napkin should be placed to the left of the dinner or service plate or across it. Both positions are correct, but for formal dinners the napkin must be placed across the service plate. When the meal is finished the napkin should be placed (never refolded) at the left of the place setting.

Fancy folds for napkins are amusing for special parties and in children's settings, but, on the whole, a plain, simple fold looks more appropriate on an elegant table. For informal settings, such as breakfast, luncheon, and afternoon tea, the triangular fold is favored. The longest side of the napkin is placed next to the forks, with the open corner away from the plate. The oblong fold is also used for luncheon, when the napkin is either to the left or across the service plate, and for buffets, when it is lined up neatly alone or with the necessary flatware. The formal dinner napkin is folded in thirds to form a rectangle, preferably not longer than the diameter of the service plate, and laid across it. If a first course must be in place on the service plate, then the napkin is placed on the left side beyond the forks.

OPPOSITE: A display vignette showing a suitable combination of beautiful design and materials, including a French Alençon lace banquet cloth, Spode's "Golden Valley" bone china banquet service, Towle's "Old Master" sterling flatware, German Rhine wine glasses, a gilt candelabrum, and a French opaline bowl with bronze-gilt cherub base to hold the flowers.

The primary rule of table setting is that all table linen must be immaculately pressed. Starching is not the chore it once was, now that spray starch is on the market. An unavoidable center crease is all that should show, and this does help one to center the cloth on the table. Creases may be avoided by rolling the cloth, when ironed, on a roll of cardboard or heavy paper. All stains should be removed before laundering or cleaning — in fact, as soon as possible after they are discovered. Linen drawers and storage closets are made more attractive by the use of old-fashioned pomanders or "clove oranges." These are easy enough to make and may be placed or hung so that their spicy smell permeates the area.

BELOW: Floral or striped scarves look elegant when little or no other pattern is used on the table. The china here is Picard's "Crescent" pattern, and the silver Oneida's "Vivant."

OPPOSITE: A Thai silk scarf sets the color scheme for an Oriental buffet. Multicolored birds hover over bouquets of orange tissue paper and cerise foil roses in gold lotus bowls. The three-tiered fortune-cookie stand and food trays are of gold lacquer. An exotic table of this kind would also be suitable for a porch or patio with informal seating, Oriental style.

BELOW: Damask table cover. Here the napkin is folded in thirds to form a rectangle approximately the diameter of the service plate.
OPPOSITE: Matching floor-length cloths were used here for both the buffet and the dining table. Velvet ribbon was added for a dual color effect, the cloth being the color of the roses and the velvet the color of the green grapes. At Christmas a red and green combination would be particularly appropriate.

ABOVE: Organdy appliquéd cloth. The napkin has a pointed fold to show the decorative corner.
BELOW: Felt tablecloths provide a wonderful color effect and background for appliqués. The wide range of available colors make them adaptable for many special occasions. They are practical, however, only when food and drink are not likely to be spilt.

Mats in various shapes, textures, and qualities have become acceptable for all occasions except for the most formal affairs and for tea tables. They are even used for small private weddings where a fully extended table and a banquet-sized cloth are rarely used.

OPPOSITE: Table runners or scarves are more decorative than mats, and they are less trouble to care for than a full tablecloth. The hourglass shape used here, to accommodate two opposite settings, and the end-of-table design for the host and hostess create an original and striking design.

ABOVE: Handwoven fiber mats have an interesting texture and are excellent for informal luncheon settings. They are available in a wide variety of colors.

RIGHT: The crocheted round mat or doily is English in origin. It was named after Thomas D'Oyly, a linen draper who traded at the Nun, a public house in Covent Garden in the seventeenth century. His small linen mats were used under bottles and finger bowls.

BELOW: Plastic mats (this one resembles fragile Venetian lace) are a practical alternative to fine linen because they are so easy to keep clean.

ABOVE: Sheet music placed under a glass cover makes an original table mat for a party centering around a musical evening.

LEFT: Hand-crocheted mats of heavy cotton that launder well and need no ironing are popular again for summer luncheons and breakfast settings.

The shape and placement of the napkin varies from one country to another. LEFT: This English setting by Wedgwood shows the napkin with four points set like sails. The dark green fitted cloth of *broderie anglaise* complements the translucent quality of fine bone china. BELOW LEFT: The decorative quality of Wedgwood's hand-embossed Queen's Ware requires a plain napkin also with a simple fold. BELOW: A napkin folded simply, to display the monogram.

RIGHT: A place setting arranged in Sweden on handcrafted linen place mats. The napkin, attractively folded, draws attention to the need to move the finger bowl and plate to their position on the left of the setting. Glasses are for champagne and sherry.

Linen as a table cover has been mentioned in the Bible and in other records that have come down to us from earliest times. It has stood for quality, luxury, and social position. Medieval paintings show covers of some fabric on all the trestle tables used in the homes of the upper classes. Serving was done from the free inner sides of these tables. During and after the Renaissance, the tablecloth began to show signs of added attention. In the illustrations on pages 58 and 74, the marks of the linen presses are obvious. On page 74 (the second picture), one can see that the cloth is artistically draped. On page 264 a knot in the corner of the cloth is puzzling, but it could be to weight the cloth down and hold it in place, or possibly the young man on the left was annoyed by its length and knotted the cloth to get it out of his way.

In Europe and England until the fifteenth century the trestle tables were removed after the meal was finished. Then, as they became more solid in construction and design, they became more permanent. In the English manor house they were placed in the hall, one on a dais for the master and his important guests, and the others down the length of the hall, lined up on either side.

In the early seventeenth century La Rochefoucauld·described dinner as one of the most wearisome of his English experiences, for it lasted from four to five hours, and he complained that "the first two are spent in eating, and you are compelled to exercise your stomach to the fullest in order to please your host." When the cloth was removed, "the most beautiful table that it is possible to see" was disclosed. All the dining tables he saw had a "brilliant polish like that of the finest glass."

The general use of fingers while eating a meal made napkins even more essential than they are today. Napkins were generous in size and, it seems, always rectangular. In sixteenth-century England napkins were "fayre folden" at each place, with a spoon tucked inside. Samuel Pepys noted in his famous diary in 1668 that he was "mightily pleased with the fellow that came to lay the cloth and fold the napkins, which I like so well, as that I am resolved to give him 40s. to teach my wife to do it."

In Europe, tablecloths as well as napkins were folded with special care. We can admire the French artistry at folding tablecloths in the seventeenth century even if it does not inspire in us an ambition to duplicate it: "First, as it is used, the tablecloth is folded and creased in France in such a manner that the square corners remain which can be folded in waves or in lozenges, but if there is a beautiful design in the cloth, then this method would not be used." In England in the same period the rough tables were covered with Turkey carpets, imported from the Near East, and, we can assume, from Turkey, over which a damask or linen cloth was spread. Later these same Turkey carpets came with English immigrants to New England. We see them illustrated in many old paintings such as the one on the following page.

A family in Holland enjoys the Twelfth Night feast in this seventeenth-century painting by Jan Steen. The child is crowned King of the festivities for finding the bean in his Christmas cake. Note the large napkins tied round the waist and neck.

OPPOSITE: "The Happy Family" by Jan Steen, painted when New York (New Amsterdam) was a Dutch settlement. Turkey carpets were used on American tables and covered with a linen or damask cloth, as shown here.
BELOW: Before forks were introduced to Europe at the beginning of the seventeenth century, fingers separated food and conveyed it to the mouth, making large napkins necessary. One is seen in this detail of the painting by Hendrick ter Brugghen below.

ABOVE: A seventeenth-century French print shows the well-marked squares on the tablecloth made by the linen press. BELOW: An eighteenth-century banquet for the installation of the Knights of St. Patrick at Dublin Castle, with a tablecloth draped in a decorative manner.

The napkin seems to have been less common in eighteenth-century England, probably owing to the fact that the fork, once an awkward tool, was now regularly used, so that eating with one's hands was unnecessary. As mentioned in Constance Spry's book, *Flower Decorations,* nineteenth-century writers tell us of "tables triumphant with the doublest of damasks, the thick and gleaming table cloths, emblems of the laundress's art, bearing napkins like galleons in full sail, with serried ranks of sparkling glasses, decanters, vases, bonbonnières . . . and perhaps arising from a large and handsome table centre an incredibly ornate crystal and silver épergne." Later, damask seems to have given way in many instances to "red plush and yellow satin trimmed with ribbon work" and "grass green satin with pen-painted daisies." Another table description mentions "a length of crimson velvet bordered with gold bullion fringe; this was 'rucked' almost the length of the table and bespattered with small cut-glass vases filled with maidenhair fern and flowers from the greenhouse." Gargantuan tables, elaborate covers, and tropical forest effects in decoration began to disappear with the industrial revolution.

Convention had been less rigid in America for some time. The few colonists who could live as they had in England and Europe were far outnumbered by the many who had no tablecloths, no china plates, and only a few knives and spoons. Both literature and art help to establish the record of those early years when immigrants, mostly from the middle classes, began the foundations for a new way of life. As already mentioned, the first tables shown in records after the Middle Ages were made from boards placed on trestles. The cover, when one was used, was called a "borde cloth." The word "tablecloth" appeared in England during the sixteenth century and although it seems to have been interchangeable with "boardcloth," nevertheless some entries indicate that there was a difference, probably developing at the time when more of the nobility had solid tables instead of, or as well as, the trestle arrangements.

American colonists brought their boards and boardcloths with them. In 1612 Alice Jones of Suffolk County, Massachusetts, had "one great tablebord" and "one short tablebord." John Winthrop, who arrived with the first colonists in Massachusetts in 1630 and was the colony's first governor, soon became aware of the important things the new settlers should bring with them and referred to them in his journal. He and others wrote back to England, saying, "Come well furnished with linnen." As it took relatively little space, it was brought in "passengers' chests, trunks, packs, and hogsheads of 'houshould stuffe.' " During the first century of colonization the records show that linen was higher in value than furniture and most other belongings. At Salem, Massachusetts, in 1664, "3 p. of sheets, 1 duzzen of napkins" were valued at three pounds, while "a table and frame, 3 chaires and three chests" were appraised at one pound five shillings.

The Metropolitan Museum of Art, New York, has a piece of damask dated 1663, from a Dutch workshop, which is well documented as a napkin. It measures 42 by 29½ inches. Napkins in this period were usually one-third the "breadth" of the cloth. In 1688 we read of "26 yards of huggabag [huckaback, a fabric of linen or cotton and linen] for making two dozen of table-napkins." Measurements were not very accurate in those days, but apparently tablecloths were of all lengths and widths. Occasionally the wealthy had a suite (also spelled "sute" or "suit") of linen for the table.

The fabrics of that era included damask, with its fine texture and handsome pictorial patterns, diaper linen, with its small, regularly repeated pattern, and holland, huckaback, canvas, and cotton. Costly damask was for the rich; diaper linen appears more often on inventories with holland and huckaback. Other inexpensive fabrics were "ozenbrig, dowlas, and lockram." In 1677 one John Paine owned "one duz hom made napkins." In 1698 the great-grandfather of George Washington had "10 old Virg'a cloth Napkins," proving that linen was now being made in America. Most of this linen was white. However, mention is to be found of "24 blew stript & wrought napkins" and a "stript table cloth." Printed linen huckaback, and "checquer'd Linnens, striped Hollands" were available in 1723.

In 1781 the Marquis de Chastellux, in his *Travels in North America in the Years 1780-82,* described a dinner at Washington's headquarters: "At our return we found a good dinner ready, and about twenty guests, among whom were General Howe and Sinclair. The repast was in the English fashion, consisting of eight or ten large dishes of butcher's meat, and poultry, with vegetables of several sorts, followed by a second course of pastry, comprised under the denominations of pies and puddings. After this the cloth was taken off, and apples and a great quantity of nuts were served."

At this time napkins disappeared for a while from the tabletop, owing to the people's dexterity with forks. In 1780 Baron Louis de Closen wrote, "Another peculiarity of this country is the absence of napkins, even in the homes of the wealthy. Napkins, as a rule, are never used and one has to wipe one's mouth on the tablecloth, which in consequence suffers in appearance." Naturally, fastidious hostesses did not tolerate this for long. In *The House Servant's Directory,* published in 1827, the author, Robert Roberts, instructed the maid to "put on your napkins, having them neatly folded so as to admit the bread into them, without being seen." After the finger glass (finger bowl) had been used, following the second course, the cloth was carefully rolled up and taken away, so that dessert could be served with wine on the bare table.

At fashionably late dinner parties in the early 1800s city ladies withdrew after the cloth was removed. The gentlemen joined them later in the parlor or drawing room for a light refreshment of fruit, biscuits or cakes, and tea, and sometimes coffee.

These colonial dinner tables were not arranged as they are today. They were "set out" or covered with platters arranged in symmetrical pattern so that little of the tablecloth was visible. Sometimes two tablecloths were used — the "nether" or second cloth is spoken of in a letter Congressman Thomas H. Hubbard of New York wrote to his wife in 1817. After a visit to Woodlawn Plantation, in Mount Vernon, Virginia, he gave this charming description of the life in that household:

> We had a light and late breakfast and dined at four. The table was spread with double table cloths, and the first course consisted of beef, mutton, oysters, soup, etc. The first cloth was removed with these viands and the clean one below was covered with pies, puddings, tarts, jellies, whips, floating island, sweetmeats, etc., and after these we came to the plain mahogany table. Clean glasses were brought on and a lighter kind of wine with fruit, raisins and almonds. We did not sit long at the table and coffee and tea were sent around at eight.

The pleasures of the table at this time and at least for the next century were the most important form of entertainment available.

A Flemish seventeenth-century linen damask napkin. It measures forty inches by twenty-nine.

An early example of the potter's art. A Cretan cup, c. 2000 B.C.

6.

Chinaware

The visual beauty of china, its design, color, and fine translucent quality took many centuries to evolve. This chapter will not recall the complete history of this evolution or of all those who contributed to the process. Only those factories which have made a special contribution to the history of china are mentioned, along with those whose products appear in the photographs in this book.

The word "chinaware" originated in England and is the present-day term applied to porcelain. The word came into use simply because the first porcelain pieces to be seen in England were from China. Today "china" is often used loosely to cover all dinnerware, even earthenware, but the two are very different, in both the material used and the texture.

The potter's art goes back to prehistoric times in Mesopotamia, Egypt, and China, long before it flourished in such Aegean lands as Crete, where recent excavations unearthed "a dinner service containing hundreds of cups, plates, warming dishes, pots and tripods, most of them made of terra cotta," dating back 3500 years. Terra cotta, still used today for earthenware, is of much coarser texture than porcelain.

OPPOSITE: Detail of a seventeenth-century fresco at Fiesole, Florence, showing a heartbroken cherub (lower right corner) in the unhappy state of not only having lost his supper but having broken his plate too.

An eighteenth-century Chinese Export Porcelain plate decorated with the insignia of the Society of the Cincinnati. This one is the rarest of the three types of Cincinnati motifs with the figure of Fame and the Fitzhugh border. It belongs to a dinner service bought by George Washington in 1786.

LEFT: The Hai Kwan Pu, or "Hoppo," as he was known in England, appointed by the Emperor of China to collect trading "duty," dines sumptuously at the expense of the British merchants.

OPPOSITE: Blue and white Canton (1784-1824) was once regarded as commonware and used as ballast in ships importing tea. Even so, its charm was appreciated by such men as George Washington and James Whistler. There used to be no identifying marks; the shapes, knobs, and decorations identified the age.

The Chinese had, to some extent, developed the art of porcelain-making by the sixth century. True porcelain, with a hard, white, translucent, and resonant body, appeared about the end of the Sung period, in the thirteenth century, but the best examples date from the Ming Dynasty, which lasted from 1368 to 1643.

In the sixteenth century European traders began to bring this ware to Europe and England. Europeans called it "porcelain" after the porcellana, a shellfish with a pearly, translucent shell. In the seventeenth century considerable quantities of china were imported into England and Europe, where it became fashionable among the aristocracy. Chinese merchants were quick to see the potentialities of this new market and their trade in the West soon began to gather momentum. Before the arrival in Europe of these delicate pieces, even kings did not possess china. They ate from plates made of gold and silver, while their richer subjects used plates of pewter, and the poorer ones, wooden trenchers.

The development of quality porcelain was slower in Japan. In the fifteenth century a Japanese potter named Shonzui visited China to study the means by which the Chinese achieved perfection in the art. Later, a Korean named Yi Sampei, who came to Japan with other Korean immigrants at the beginning of the seventeenth century, is credited with the discovery of deposits of earth suitable for making porcelain, in a remote village called Kutani, in the Arita area. Porcelain produced in that region, known as "Old Kutani," was made on commission for the landed nobles from about 1650 to 1700. The first pieces were heavy and imperfect but were wonderfully decorated. Later, the best pieces were acknowledged to rival anything produced in the Far East. Although inspired by Chinese models, the finest Japanese porcelain of the seventeenth and eighteenth centuries was quite different.

As opposed to the subtleties that distinguished Chinese ware, the Kutani potters loved flamboyant color and geometric and edge-to-edge designs that were often patterned after old brocades.

The Arita district produced several kinds of porcelain, perhaps the best known of which are Kakiemon, Imari, and Nabeshima. Kakiemon, the potter who was born in 1596 and lived until 1666, founded a new art of enameling. Kaki, the color of a ripe persimmon, was so much favored that Kakiemon is supposed to have added this word to his name. The enameled wares developed during this period made his name, style, and school synonymous with Japanese porcelain.

Imari, the seaport for Arita, gave its name to the porcelain from this area, which was generally elaborately decorated. Color was used for its own sake and not to duplicate nature; thus we see red water, green flowers, blue trees, and other such phenomena. Imari porcelain was mass-produced for export.

Nabeshima porcelain, on the other hand, was produced in smaller quantity for a more discriminating clientele, at the beginning of the eighteenth century. This clientele included the first families of Japan, and for over a century formal tables were set in matching pieces that had to be duplicated by the artists. To meet this almost impossible demand the technique of decoration-transfer was evolved, which helps explain the remarkable uniformity observed in good Nabeshima. Owing to the high standard maintained, the Nabeshima that exists today is almost always of good quality.

The Japanese affection for genre treatments of familiar and revered subjects asserts itself from time to time, and this strong undercurrent deep in all Japanese art makes it recognizable to the interested eye. Kakiemon and Imari were both later reproduced in England. In the seventeenth century the Dutch persuaded the Japanese to allow them trading privileges, and these they held for two hundred years. The Dutch East India Company imported almost forty-five thousand pieces of Japanese porcelain into Holland. Kyoto had many artisans of great ability and good taste from the middle of the eighteenth century onward. Today, the largest centers of modern Japanese porcelain in production are found in the vicinity of Kyoto, Nagoya, and Arita.

The initial impetus to the general introduction of china into everyday life began in the seventeenth century, when tea-drinking became fashionable. Mugs and tankards of pewter, silver, and heavy pottery had been used for ale, a popular beverage, but these would not do for hot tea. Fashion prescribed dainty cups of porcelain for this exotic new drink. A more practical reason for using porcelain was that the subtleties of the tea's taste and fragrance were destroyed when it was drunk from vessels of other materials. The first porcelain cups were small, for tea was expensive. They were also made without handles, as the Chinese designed them for their own use this way. Handles were added later as a concession to foreign demand, but even in the nineteenth century teacups followed the Chinese design and were sold without handles. The old table services of silver and pewter were not immediately abandoned but people became aware of the elegance and fascination of chinaware and soon it became fashionable to own and use it. Thus teacups and their related equipage helped acquaint the world with the worth and desirability of china.

The famous East India Companies, which played such a highly important role in introducing tea to the West, naturally became involved in bringing the proper china cups and saucers, teapots, and plates in their ships. This china was called Chinese Export Porcelain, because it was, in fact, porcelain made in China for export. It varied greatly in quality, from eggshell with an almost white, even glaze, to heavier ware with a decidedly gray cast and uneven surface. The decoration, too, was varied, and manufacturers in the Western world began to copy it as soon as they discovered the much-guarded secret of porcelain-making and were able to produce such pieces themselves.

By the middle of the nineteenth century the quality of Chinese porcelain had begun to decline. Some Chinese Export Porcelain, decorated with European motifs, came, through accident, to be known as Oriental Lowestoft, for there was a factory producing china at Lowestoft, in England. Oriental Lowestoft, made in China to the order of foreign merchants and decorated with European motifs, is rarely found today outside museums. Only fine reproductions are on the market today.

Beautiful china in a great variety of designs has been available for so long that we are inclined to take it for granted. Our seventeenth- and eighteenth-century forebears, however, were enthralled by the wondrous quality of Chinese porcelain, and they recognized the great skill of the Chinese potters' art. The secret of its making had to be found out, and every prospective European manufacturer sooner or later became involved one way or another in this pursuit. The excitement, the urgency, and the competition must have been intense.

In Europe, the credit for discovering the secret of making hard-paste porcelain goes to Johann Böttger. As a young German living in Berlin, he showed great aptitude for chemistry and became an apothecary's apprentice; later he was transferred to Saxony, and in 1709 he found a successful formula.

In 1710 a porcelain factory was set up by royal patent in the castle of Albrechtsburg, overlooking the town of Meissen, a few miles from Dresden. To begin with, the development was jealously guarded, and the workmen were employed virtually as prisoners. However, as time went on, it was inevitable that some of the workmen should be lured from Meissen and the secrets of the craft were soon known to all the best factories in Europe. In 1863 the Meissen factory was moved from the old fortress. Great commercial advancement followed, but the finest and most distinctive period of Meissen was drawing to an end. The term "Meissen" is applied to productions of the royal factory during the classical period (1720-1820). Later works of the royal factory and other porcelains made in Dresden are termed "Dresden."

An epoch-making event in the history of Chinese porcelain was the production of the enormous family of blue-and-white ware which dates back to the fourteenth century. Introduction of this ware into Europe found many imitators. In Germany, Meissen's "onion" or Strohblumen pattern later was copied by Royal Copenhagen to the extent that this blue-and-white design became known as "Copenhagen."

Although Holland made some very good china, it seems to be best known for its underglaze delft pottery. The name comes from the Dutch town of Delft, where, from the seventeenth century on, delft earthenware dishes were made in great quantity. The term "delftware" is generically applied to English wares, too, referring to those made of coarse native clay. The same kind of ware in France is called "faïence," and in Italy, "majolica." Delftware was the potters' contribution for people who could not afford true porcelain.

In 1745, England had some small successes in producing china. Chelsea and Bow, which developed at this time, were greatly influenced by the products of the Chinese, Japanese, Germans, and French. About this period, Staffordshire potters developed a fine white earthenware that was called creamware. In 1770 delftware gave way to the more practical creamware, now a commercial success through Josiah Wedgwood's exacting standards of design and technique. The elegance and utility of creamware made it a serious rival to the more expensive porcelain, and its acceptance in society was established when Queen Charlotte gave it her patronage and Wedgwood changed the name to "Queen's Ware." The prestige accorded to Wedgwood led to one of his most remarkable achievements, the creation of a creamware dinner service of 952 items, each painted with a different English view, which he supplied to Catherine II, Empress of Russia, in 1775. Wedgwood was one of the two most successful apprentices of Thomas Whieldon, considered the most ingenious potter in England. Josiah Spode the elder was the other. In 1789 he began the factory at Stoke-on-Trent, which continues today under the name of Spode-Copeland.

Other factories, such as the potters of Leeds, began making fine-quality creamware, copying one another's designs, and their enormous success in Europe forced Continental potters to follow suit. The widespread British success revolutionized the development of European earthenware in the second half of the eighteenth century. Although European earthenware was made of coarser material, some of the decorations had a special charm and sophistication.

After delft, creamware, and queensware came still another attempt to imitate porcelain. In 1806 Spode invented a felspathic earthenware which he called "stone china." This was so near an approximation of porcelain, and its texture was so much finer than that of other earthenware, that it immediately captured the public's fancy. It was ideal for old Chinese designs in brilliant enamels, and effects could be produced which were impossible with other earthenware. This semiporcelain ironstoneware is still in production. Spode's stoneware pattern called "George Washington at Mount Vernon," which is available today, is an exact copy of the original Chinese Export Ware used by the first American President at Mount Vernon.

A collection of early eighteenth- and nineteenth-century Meissen includes a large fish platter, a sauce boat, footed soup dishes with cover and handle, sweetmeat dishes (used for pepper and salt here), and matching knife rests. Knife rests, used between courses, were put on many tables in the eighteenth century to support the one knife, but they are now made in silver and glass and used mainly for carving sets.

At this time, Spode's development of a formula for using calcined bones in the paste produced a strong, practical body that rivaled the beautiful wares of the Orient. This procedure was adopted by the famous English firms of Worcester, Wedgwood, Minton, and Doulton, who, with Spode, are the only makers of English bone china. Stoke-on-Trent in Staffordshire eventually became the pottery center of England and possibly of the entire modern world. "The Potteries" and English bone china have become synonymous to those seeking fine craftsmanship for tableware.

Whereas the early Spode motifs reflected a strong Chinese influence, the Wedgwood patterns and shapes were distinctly classical in feeling. Wedgwood's neat stylized borders and naturalistic effects were novel at that time, inasmuch as they broke away from imitation of the Chinese and European designs.

The Worcester Porcelain Company manufactured a china body in 1751. In the next twenty-five years Dr. John Wall had a great influence on the development of the company, which produced an extremely popular blue and white tableware inspired by the Chinese porcelain. In the *Oxford Journal* in 1763 they advertised: "Services of Chinese porcelain can be made up with Worcester porcelain, so that the differences cannot be discovered." And this they did (see opposite). In 1783 Thomas Flight took over the firm. In 1793 Martin Barr entered the picture and Flight & Barr was established; in 1802 the firm became known as Barr, Flight and Barr. Finally in 1840, through amalgamation, the Royal Worcester Porcelain Company was set up and continues in operation to the present day.

Doulton & Watts, now known as Royal Doulton, began in 1815 when John Doulton and John Watts acquired an interest in a factory in Lambeth. After five years they became the owners and soon moved to larger premises. In 1854 John Watts retired and the firm became known as Doulton & Co. John's son Henry had the energy and ability to develop the business further by adding new factories to make earthenware, etc., and by developing a decorative-art department at Lambeth. In 1884 a new wing was added for the manufacture of bone china. The company's distinctive contributions in the field of ceramic painting on decorative pottery and porcelain soon led to a deservedly high reputation, and today it has added modern design to its ever-popular range of patterns.

Tableware has always been the main product of Minton China, a famous factory begun in 1798. Other important English china factories still operating include Royal Crown Derby and Coalport. Caughley, a factory absorbed by Coalport, also claims our attention because probably no other establishment did more to popularize blue-printed china. The "willow pattern," an imitation of Chinese Cantonware known the world over, emanated from Caughley about 1780 and has since been copied by almost every English factory.

Several china factories were founded in Limoges, in France, about 1783, and the one called Haviland is still in production. It was not until 1839 that an American, David Haviland, decided to settle in France with his American wife to make porcelain for the American market. David's son Theodore contributed much to the growth and fame that followed, and his great-grandson, another Theodore, is today president of the factory in Limoges that produces Haviland china.

Sèvres is another French factory of great interest. Sèvres china dates from 1756 and is still in production, owing, it would seem, not only to its unparalleled excellence and beauty but to the good taste of Madame de Pompadour and the financial support and patronage of King Louis XV. The factory remains a great national institution, having contributed much to the porcelain art.

Medici china was produced in a factory in the Boboli Gardens, Florence, in 1580, un-

OPPOSITE: Porcelain made c. 1760 by Royal Worcester.

86

der the tutelage of the Grand Duke of Tuscany. This ware never achieved the fame and importance of Meissen, and today there are fewer than fifty authentic pieces in existence. Italy, however, is well represented by Ginori and Capo di Monte.

In 1735 the Marchese Carlo Ginori founded a factory in Doccia, outside Florence; this is one of the few early European factories not sponsored by royalty but supported by the original efforts of the founder. The factory museum there testifies to great competence in fine porcelain-making handed down from one generation to the next.

In 1743 the Capo di Monte factory was established by Charles III, King of Naples. When he left Naples for Madrid in 1759 he took with him the best models, molds, and workmen. King Ferdinand IV, however, reopened the factory in Portici in 1771, and then later on it was re-established in Naples, where it remained until it closed in 1821, after it had sold many of its molds to Ginori with the right to use the Capo di Monte mark on the reproductions.

Royal Copenhagen china, begun in 1756 with the help of a former Dresden modeler, continues to operate today. Flora Danica (see page 35), originally planned as a gift for Catherine the Great of Russia, is an interpretation in porcelain of an eighteenth-century book of that name, which was a botanical classic. With the book plates as a guide, more than a thousand pieces were made over a period of thirteen years. By the time the set was complete Catherine had died, and so in 1803 it was accepted by the Danish Royal Family. It is the only eighteenth-century royal banquet service still in production. This Danish company was also fond of decorations in blue and white, and the Strohblumen and "onion" patterns borrowed from Dresden were great favorites, and remain so today.

Following Meissen and Dresden in Germany came two famous German companies: Nymphenburg and Berlin China. Nymphenburg made German tableware and food warmers, starting in 1747 under the Elector of Bavaria. Today, in private hands, it continues to produce beautiful pieces. Berlin China, which started in 1750 and continues to produce, made excellent tableware inspired by Meissen. When King Frederick the Great took over the company in 1763, he employed drastic measures for its success; he held lotteries and decreed that no Jew could obtain a marriage certificate until he had purchased a set of Berlin china. Some pieces of Old Berlin are shown on the top shelves in the picture on page 230.

A more modern German factory of interest to table-setters today is Rosenthal, founded in 1879. With a team of international designers, this firm now exports its wide variety of china to more than eighty countries. Flatware and glassware have been added to correlate with table settings (see page 94).

Most of the chinaware in use in America in the first half of the nineteenth century came from England or was imported from the East. England produced earthenware and

OPPOSITE: Haviland porcelain plates, made in Limoges, France, c. 1900. The Dresden candelabra and the large napkins belong to the same period.

ABOVE: President Wilson ordered this service for the White House in 1918. It was the first American-made dinnerware to be ordered by a President and was part of a seventeen-hundred-piece Lenox set executed in cobalt blue with an outer border of etched gold.

stone china, transfer-printed in dark blue with American buildings, views, and public personages. Many shiploads arrived in the United States, and numerous collections may be seen in museums and historical houses now open to the public. The habits and traditions of the early settlers were reflected in their preference for imported wares. The independent English potters catered for the new middle class with practical wares, in contrast to the great European potteries, mostly controlled by royalty, which produced fine wares beyond the reach of the frugal colonists.

Before and after the Revolution, coarse red and brown glazed pottery was made locally of native clay and often peddled from door to door. The thrifty New Englander saved her "imports" and used mostly the red clayware with wooden trenchers and pewter. When the boycott on English goods lifted in the 1780s, Leeds earthenware and Wedgwood creamware were imported in great quantities. Wedgwood's creamware (or queensware as it was later known) was so plentiful and inexpensive that it crowded pewter and other tableware off the market. Newspaper advertisements of public sales about this time listed many and varied tablewares under the English word "crockery," which, of course, is still used by the British today. The most popular was "blew and white": either English Caughley's willow pattern earthenware or Chinese Canton porcelain.

Canton was one of the Chinese Export Porcelain patterns which originally came to

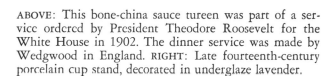

ABOVE: This bone-china sauce tureen was part of a service ordered by President Theodore Roosevelt for the White House in 1902. The dinner service was made by Wedgwood in England. RIGHT: Late fourteenth-century porcelain cup stand, decorated in underglaze lavender.

America via England because of the East India Company's monopoly of the trade. After the Revolution, in 1784, the first American ship, *Empress of China*, set up direct trade, which continued for the next forty years, supplying all the Chinese porcelain the East Coast of the United States could desire. Canton was named after the Chinese port from which it was shipped. Most of it was painted by hand in Canton. It was inexpensive, heavy, and so plentiful that it was used as ballast in ships bringing tea from China, and so it is easy to understand why it was regarded as "commonware." However, George Washington found it to his taste — as the Mount Vernon collection testifies — and people living inland, where it was no doubt harder to come by, also appreciated its addition to the "setting out" of the table.

So much early reference to Canton makes it interesting to collect, but its charm lies also in the endless variation of design, for no two pieces are the same unless they happen to have been done by the same artist. The design often shows a bridge over water, a Chinese house, a willow tree, etc., in typical Chinese manner. Nanking has finer decoration and more elaborate borders, as does Fitzhugh, another type of Canton. There were no identifying marks; the shapes, knobs, grade of porcelain, and decorations identify the age or period.

America's first efforts seem to have started with the son of one Benjamin Tucker, a

Philadelphia Quaker who produced Philadelphia China from 1825 to 1838. His china had the advantage of being able to withstand a higher degree of heat than the Sèvres hard-paste porcelain for which it was frequently mistaken.

Little china other than the Philadelphia variety was made in America prior to 1840. Sometime around 1858 the Onondaga Pottery Company, Syracuse, New York, came into existence. It was not until 1893 that it produced china suitable for the table. The company was the first to develop its own ceramic decalcomanias, and today it has one of the finest lithographic departments in the industry. In 1889 in Trenton, New Jersey, an important pottery center in the New World, Walter Scott Lenox became a partner in the Ceramic Art Company. In 1894 he became sole owner and in 1906 formed Lenox Incorporated. At the turn of the century Lenox had slowly developed his own formula and was soon making fine china dinnerware comparable to the best. Still it was a long, uphill fight to convince Americans, strongly prejudiced in favor of the famous European and English china names and the inexpensive Chinese imports, that fine dinnerware could be made in their own country.

Then in 1918 Woodrow Wilson ordered a seventeen-hundred-piece Lenox dinner set for the White House; he was the first Chief Executive to purchase American china. Foreign firms still dominated the domestic market: eight out of every ten pieces sold were imports. It was not until some fifteen years later, when Lenox introduced a new modern style, that the breakaway from English and European tradition really began. Its clean, simple line was in contrast to the elaborate heavy florals and often rococo style that had been so popular. Lenox is the only American china company producing crystal for the dining table.

World War II had its effect on imports and many American firms, including Pickard, Franciscan, Syracuse, Flintridge, and others, began to grow with the new market. The Pickard China Company is a family-owned organization which was established in 1898 when Wilder A. Pickard founded a china-decorating studio in Chicago. His designs were applied to imported blanks until 1937, when his son began the complete production of Pickard chinaware. This china has gradually changed from the hand-painted designs made famous by the original studio to the simple, contemporary patterns that have great appeal to the young brides of today. From 1943 onwards, the American market went largely domestic and it is unlikely that English and European firms will ever again have the complete domination and control they once had. Although Europe and Britain were more than a century ahead in establishing the lead in earthenware and china, America's progress today in making fine dinnerware is a definite challenge to competitors overseas.

In porcelain production, modern methods of profitable large-scale production have overcome the high cost of skilled labor, which is 70 per cent of the cost of fine chinaware. The old system of selling chinaware by the set has given way to the new approach of selling it by the place setting, as it is needed.

CHINA AND EARTHENWARE TERMS

Earthenware

Earthenware, or pottery, covers a wide range, from the crudest prehistoric examples to the elegant tableware we know today. It is opaque. It is fired twice — once to set the body, and the second time, the glaze. All earthenware except stoneware is fired at a lower temperature than china and its cost is therefore less. It is made of the same general ingredients used in china, but the proportions are different and its manufacturing process is much simpler, less exacting, and therefore quicker. It is porous and lends itself easily to color — the bright, gay, intense color that you do not see in fine china. Earthenware is made of cruder clays than china. It includes cream-colored earthenware, or queensware, salt glaze, stoneware, and ironstone. Italian majolica, French faïence, and Dutch delft also fall into this category.

This table setting, made in England, shows Wedgwood's bone china pattern "Ruby Whitehall."

Chinaware

China, or chinaware, has evolved from the potter's wheel. It is porcelain — the highest, most advanced expression of the potter's art. It is translucent. It is usually fired twice — the second time at a very intense heat. The carefully refined clays produce a strong, nonporous, vitreous surface which is resistant to chipping and is not subject to crazing. China differs from earthenware in its translucency, flawless surface, and clear glaze. China is di-

LEFT: Five members from the Rosenthal Studio team combined their talents for this setting. Hans Theo Baumann of Germany produced the "Linear" shape of the china. Count Emilio Pucci of Italy decorated it with his "Veneto" pattern. The crystal soup bowl and sterling silver are by Tapio Wirkkala of Finland, the stemware is by Claus Josef Riedel of Austria, and the tulip-shaped candlesticks are by Bjørn Wiinblad of Denmark.

RIGHT: Oxford bone china, made in America today incorporates all the qualities of true porcelain. It is pure white and translucent, and, although exquisitely thin, it has the strength needed for daily use. This blue pattern called "Bryn Mawr" is rimmed in platinum.

LEFT: Early in the 20th century the American firm of Lenox introduced a new style of china. Its clean, simple lines, in contrast to elaborate florals, marked the beginning of a new era in porcelain design. This pattern, "Tableau," has a rich mosaic motif in green, beige, and Pompeiian red.

RIGHT: A modern design from California is Franciscan's "Encanto" pattern, in plain white, set on a brown linen cloth by John Matouk. The stemware is by Dorothy Thorpe.

vided into three groups: soft-paste, hard-paste, and bone china, which is between soft-paste and hard-paste. Bone china, as the name implies, contains calcined bone dust.

Ceramics

Ceramics is a general term applied to anything made from baked clay.

Dinnerware and Tableware

These are the two general terms to apply to plates made of any and every material. "China" should be used only when referring to porcelain, but "chinaware" is generally accepted today as a general term for dinnerware.

These two pages show a china pattern, with the ever-popular rose motif, used in three different settings created in Australia: for a family dinner, a buffet, and (below) a supper party, when a lettuce basket filled with green apples and decorated with a pink bow was used as the centerpiece on a pink and white checked cloth; the pattern is "Camelot Rose" by Johnson Brothers.

COLLECTION AND SELECTION OF CHINA

The more we understand about china the more we appreciate and enjoy it. Collecting old china is a fascinating hobby, and one that can make table setting an exciting experience. With every piece something comes to us from history, and often this is picturesquely recorded in one way or another on the china itself.

In identifying china there are many fine books available as guides. However, so much in design overlaps from one period to another and from one factory to another, and so much was borrowed or copied, that expert advice is often needed to identify it properly. The final decision on the origin cannot always be made by the "back stamp," or mark. This is known to have been deliberately forged sometimes or made to resemble very closely marks belonging to another factory, or to have been applied after the date of manufacture. But if an old piece delights you it hardly matters whether the back stamp is authentic or not.

Selecting china is a question of personal taste, governed by finances. Acquisition of old china might come through years of collecting or through inheritance. Whether or not it comes to us in sets is not necessarily of prime importance. The service plates can be of one kind, while the soup dishes may be of another pattern, provided that they harmonize in color and design. Dessert and coffee service, however, always seem more attractive when they do match. When a buffet is used for food service, the meat platter, vegetable dishes, and gravy boat may be another collection. Breakfast and luncheon sets are usually less formal and can be collected in smaller numbers.

Modern china from well-established firms is usually selected from patterns listed as "open stock," which means that individual replacements or additions may be purchased separately. Some patterns have been sold for generations, while others are popular enough to be guaranteed for ten years or more. Naturally patterns are manufactured only as long as they are in demand. A closed set of china has a given number of pieces; single pieces are never sold. Even in modern china, dessert plates and tea-and-coffee services are sometimes chosen in another harmonizing pattern.

Earthenware can be correlated in a free manner. Place settings may harmonize or contrast in color — or a plain color may be used with a decorated service plate selected because of its complementary hues. Texture and color play a greater role in setting informal tables with earthenware.

Starter sets consist of twenty pieces, for four place settings. Naturally the amount of china you need will be decided by your way of life, the amount of entertaining you do, and the size of your family.

OPPOSITE: Wedgwood's "Charnwood" pattern determined the color scheme for this setting for luncheon on a terrace. The bouquet of flowers is seen through the glass top of the table. The crystal is by Fostoria, the sterling flatware by Gorham.

CHINA CARE AND STORAGE

This will determine the life span of a set, proper treatment prolonging its use indefinitely. The most frequent cause of breakage is uneven application of heat. China must be warmed gradually and evenly and never put directly on a hot stove. A warm plate is necessary for hot food, but a plate should never be so hot that it is necessary to use asbestos mats to protect a table.

Hot soapy water is recommended as the best cleaner. Harsh abrasives, especially those containing soda, should be avoided. It is inadvisable to allow china or earthenware to soak in soapy water for any length of time. China must always be thoroughly dry before being stored. Pineapple and lemon juices and vinegar may damage the sheen of some colors, so china used for these foods should be washed as soon as possible. American-made china is underglaze and can be safely washed in a machine with the special detergents recommended.

OPPOSITE: Royal Worcester's china pattern "Lavinia" enhances this table set with flowers in lavender, pink, and blue, and combined with the candles, Belgian lace, and English crystal in Stuart's "Ariel" pattern, makes a charming setting.

RIGHT: Early designs continue to be fashionable, as seen in Royal Worcester's "Reverie" pattern, which shows the Oriental style that influenced this company in the eighteenth century.

Proper, convenient storage is essential in a busy house. The rubber racks designed for this purpose make it possible to extract one piece easily without touching the others. If pieces are stacked they should be placed, not slid, one on top of another. Fine china should have either cotton felt or paper pads between each plate for protection, particularly if the pattern is overglaze or has metallic decoration. Cups should be set individually on shelves or hung on hooks.

French eighteenth-century
silver mustard pot.

7.
Silverware

Flatware is not a very prepossessing name to give to the tools with which we eat, but it is generally accepted in America and other countries by the makers of knives, spoons, and forks, no matter what the material. Many people still call their tools silverware because originally their tableware was sterling silver. In England and other English-speaking countries, cutlery is the accepted term, for it was originally the cutler who made, sharpened, repaired, and sold knives made of silver.

The history of these tools is rich in tradition. Long before man knew how to fashion metal into useful objects, at a time when primitive man lived by the sea, he used shells as tools for eating. Eventually he added wooden or bone handles for further convenience and so our first tool, the spoon, came into being. Some of our spoons today, particularly those with a shell-shaped bowl, look much like those early tools. Then, some four thousand years ago, when the Egyptian civilization was highly developed and the process of mineral refining was becoming understood, spoons were made of silver. They also were made out of one piece of wood, or carved out of slate or ivory.

The earliest reference to the making of a spoon in precious metal is in the twenty-fifth chapter of the Book of Exodus, where the Lord commands Moses to make golden spoons for the tabernacle. The Greeks and Romans made the spoon chiefly in bronze, and later in gold. Ancient spoons have been found dating from a period long before knives and forks began to appear.

The knife seems to have begun as a clumsy stone implement, used only for hunting. Then as knowledge progressed, it was made of bronze, iron, and steel. Although the knife may have been used for eating in ancient times, it is not until the Middle Ages that we have evidence of its being used for both hunting and eating.

The fork, as a weapon, is well known to everyone because of its association with such mythological characters as Triton, Neptune, and the Devil himself. Metal serving forks are known to have been used as early as 600 A.D.; possibly something of the kind was used even earlier to hold food over a fire.

Around the year 1400, when people carried their eating utensils with them, a folding silver spoon was made to fit the pocket. Later a fork was added. Even the wealthy did not provide these utensils; only royalty seem to have had enough for their feasts and banquets. Everyone carried his knife in a scabbard fastened to his belt, to use at mealtime and on any other occasion when a knife was needed. Those who could not afford silver used spoons, knives, and forks of pewter. Copper and brass spoons were used, too, by persons of limited means, although copper soon lost favor due to its tendency to rapid oxidation. During the fifteenth and sixteenth centuries, in the Tudor period, it was fashionable to give a christening gift of twelve spoons, each adorned with a miniature statue in silver of one of the twelve apostles. Sometimes a "Master" spoon bearing the figure of Christ was included. These sets are exceedingly rare today. Our "pitcher spoon" originated in Elizabethan days, when great starched ruffles were worn around the neck, making long-handled spoons a necessity.

In Italy in the 1500s knives and forks generally appeared on the tables of the cultured, but it was another century before they were popular in France and England. At one time in England it was considered effeminate to use a fork and it took several decades for the

Ancient spoons. From left to right: Bronze, Grecian; 2500-3000 years old. Brass, early Christian; 1600-1900 years old. Silver, Egyptian; 3000-4000 years old. Bronze, Greek; 2000-2500 years old. Brass, early Roman; 2500 years old. Gold, late Etruscan period; 2500 years old. Silver, ancient Roman; found in England.

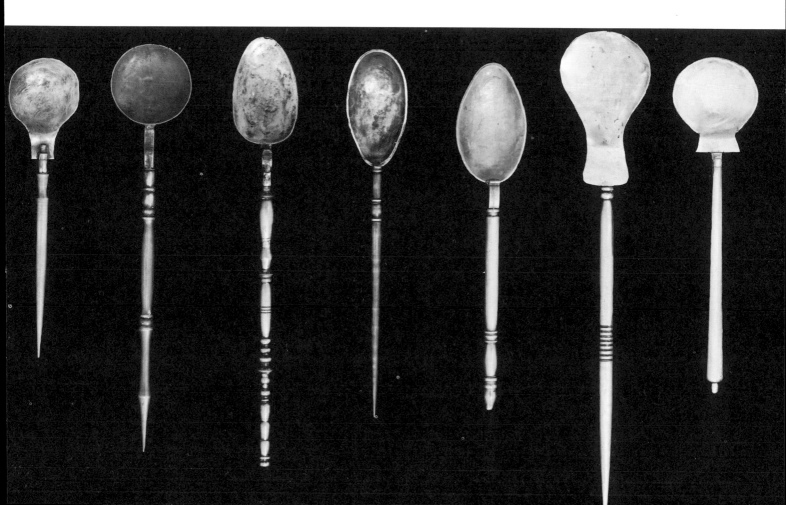

people other than the upper classes to adopt it. The clergy even protested its use "as a substitute for God-given fingers." In America, too, forks were freakish novelties: when the first fork was imported by Governor Winthrop in 1633, people thought it comical. They could not see any need for it, since most of their meats were cut up and cooked in ragouts and stews. Recipes of the time called for meat to be "y-mynced, hewed on a gobbet, hacked, diced and skerned." Two-pronged forks to spear food were the most commonly used at first, but early models were made with three and four prongs too.

Corrosion has taken a heavy toll of the ancient knives; very few specimens are found dating earlier than the sixteenth century. One of the first table knives had a broad, spatulate end to the blade, opposite the cutting edge, recommended "for the eating of pease and jelleys." Another typical blade form was broad at the shoulder, tapering to the point. The point was fine for spearing food and for conveying it to the mouth. Knives were sharp and pointed during most of the seventeenth century, and were used for killing, cutting, and carving meat as well as for eating it. Not for reasons of danger but for those of etiquette, apparently, the knife lost its sharp point. Cardinal Richelieu reportedly was disturbed by a guest who habitually picked his teeth with the point of his knife. He thus urged Louis XIV to order that all knives be rounded, which the King did. The French fashion eventually was adopted in England and thus, in the American colonies in 1669, as a means of preventing dinner-table assassinations. Once knives had begun to play a definite

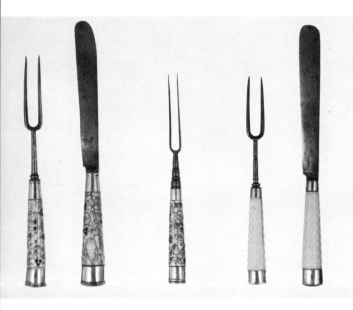

ABOVE: From left to right: Three ivory handles stained red and green with inlaid floral designs in silver wire; 1698. Knife and fork with ivory handles; late seventeenth century.

RIGHT: Collection of knives. From left to right: 1866; dredged from the River Thames. Mid-sixteenth century. Second half of sixteenth century. Late sixteenth century.

A seventeenth-century English traveling set consisting of knife, fork, and spoon with silver handles, carried in a shagreen case.

part in our eating customs the old steel knives were duplicated, but with only the blade of steel, and the handle of silver, as is common today. In the time of King James I the finest knives in the world were made in London. The handle now became a work of art, in ivory, amber, horn, jet, silver, or enamel. Hard stones such as jasper, agate, bloodstone, rock crystal, and cornelian were also used.

Traveling sets of knife, fork, and spoon were still being carried at the end of the seventeenth century. The Victoria and Albert Museum's booklet on sixteenth- to eighteenth-century English cutlery pictures some handsome silver-handled sets in shagreen cases. In the seventeenth century, spoons were made in two parts. The bowl and handles were cast, then joined by a mechanical device called a rattail; today the rattail is an integral part of many designs.

Knives and forks were in universal use by 1770 and the question was not whether to have them, but how to use them. Forks with two, three, and four tines were being used; their handles were of wood, bone (sometimes stained green), and occasionally ivory. The eighteenth century produced the pistol-shaped handle, which is seen on flatware today. Toward the close of the century, knife handles of china, earthenware, and green-stained ivory came into fashion, and these still survive in great numbers. Wooden-handled knives and forks were very cheap, and therefore the most commonly used. It was an elegant table indeed that boasted silver-hafted knives and forks.

Before the invention of stainless steel, a knife did not have a long life. Repeated cleaning and grinding soon wore away the blade, and unless the handle was made of precious material, the knife was then thrown away. In the nineteenth century, industrial methods of manufacture put an end to individually designed cutlery; production has since conformed to one of a few standard types.

There is no place in the home where a woman reveals herself more quickly than at the dining-room table. The choice and use of everything expresses her taste, or lack of it. The soft patina of old, cared-for silverware represents the pride of more than one generation. This pride in the ownership of silver originated in the Renaissance, when it was considered more valuable than gold. At that time banks were not yet used for safe-keeping and one way of accumulating wealth was to collect fine silver ornaments (including a Cellini masterpiece when possible).

Time and care should be taken in choosing a flatware pattern that will go happily with whatever dinnerware one might choose to use, for it is to be enjoyed for a lifetime. Some of the most beautiful designs to come down to us are those from the Georgian era, that were inspired by the sea. During the seventeenth century there arose a wealthy new merchant class, whose fortunes were founded on the sailing ship. These men built great estates and furnished them with all available luxuries. We find a tremendous amount of nautical derivation in all decorations of these homes, including the silver. The gadroon motif so prevalent in eighteenth-century Georgian silver is obviously derived from the ship's rope. Then, in the time of George III, there appeared two other motifs derived from the sea: the "shell" and the "dolphin." Architecture has had its influence too: the famous English architect Robert Adam left us a treasure in silverware. On the lighter side, you may today come across a well-known pattern called "Jack Shepherd." Sometimes he has been mistaken for a famous early English silversmith! Actually, of course, he was a bandit and highwayman. Although he was hanged at the early age of twenty-one years, he was famous for his ability to escape, which earned him the title of "the runaway." At this time (about 1701) footed silver came into vogue, in gravy boats, salts and peppers, bowls, coffeepots, etc. People jokingly said that these pieces had legs so they could run away like Jack Shepherd.

The first patterns and designs used by American silversmiths were of English and European origin. In New England naturally the English influence was felt, in New York the Dutch, and in Florida the Spanish. The Huguenots' influence was felt wherever they settled. Prior to the Civil War in America two basic styles prevailed; the simple, plain design, influenced by Puritanism, and the more elaborate, derived from English patterns. Many of these early designs were so beautiful that they are still being copied. Authentic reproductions of eighteenth-century museum pieces are available on our present-day market. One firm recently offered copies of a Georgian salad spoon, fork, and ladle, all of rattail design, originally made in London in 1740.

"Paul Revere" by J. S. Copley. Although many fine craftsmen contributed to American silversmithing, folklore has made Paul Revere more famous than his contemporaries.

An eighteenth-century painting by an anonymous English artist shows English silver and a blue porcelain tea set, with handleless cups.

HOLLOWARE

Holloware consists of articles given shape by spinning and turning, such as teapots and coffeepots, water pitchers, vases, gravy and sauce boats, candelabra, bowls, salt and pepper shakers, goblets, etc. There are two distinct classes, or grades, of material used. The most desirable and consequently most expensive silver-plated holloware is spun, or drawn, from highly refined nickel silver. This metal, which is nearly as precious as silver, possesses the right quality for amalgamation with pure silver. Brittaniaware, which is composed of tin, antimony, and copper, is far less durable than nickel silver. Nickel-silver holloware is easily distinguished from Britanniaware by the clear, bell-like ring it emits when tapped lightly with the fingers or a pencil.

The coffeepot and teapot are probably used more often than any other pieces of holloware; both have an interesting history. The coffeepot was derived from the early English tankard, from which coffee was served when first introduced. The first converted tankard had a round S-shaped pipe inserted into a low hole on the side that would be near for a right-handed person. These are still made in pewter reproductions today. This style would not do for left-handed persons, however, so the spout was later moved around opposite the

108

handle, where it is today. The first silver teapot was based on low, round "ball-shaped" china teapots the early traders brought back from India and China. These origins explain why the coffeepot is always taller than the teapot.

Sterling silver is one of the most useful and highly esteemed metals in our civilization. This term had its origin in the Middle Ages when silver coin was minted by German merchants trading with England. These merchants from the mainland of Europe were called "Easterlings." Their coin, 92.5 per cent silver and 7.5 per cent copper, was known as sterling. The word sterling came to mean honesty and integrity, owing to the standard character of this coin. The percentage of silver and copper established in twelfth-century coins are the standard for sterling today. Solid silver is much too soft for practical purposes, but with copper added it becomes hard enough to stand all kinds of wear. Down through the ages the percentage of pure silver in "solid" silver has varied greatly, since the amount of copper added was up to the silversmith. Not until 1300, by decree of Edward I of England, was there a definite standard. By the King's edict it was established that "no manner of vessel or server depart out of the maker's hands until it can be assayed by the warden of the craft, and further that it be stamped with a leopard's head." This explains why English silver ranks high with collectors all over the world and is a proud household possession.

Americans started using the term sterling about the middle of the nineteenth century. However it was not until 1907, six hundred years after Edward I made his decree, that President Theodore Roosevelt signed the National Stamping Law, which provides that all silverware marked "sterling" must contain 925 parts silver and 75 parts alloyed metal.

Why has silver remained the first choice for fine tableware? There are many reasons, apart from its illustrious background. It is the most hygienic metal known to man; it does not give off substances that affect the taste of foods or stain them. It adjusts instantly to temperature changes, so that there is no harsh contrast with the food it carries to the mouth. It is hard and very wear-resistant when slightly alloyed, yet it gives the impression of softness; this in turn makes it more appropriate than gold or platinum. Also, the workability of silver — the range of finishes possible to it — gives designers and craftsmen great creative latitude. Furthermore, because the metal causes reflected light to become softly diffused, silver gives off a deep, warm, luminous glow.

Sterling silver is a precious metal that lasts forever and indeed grows more beautiful with the passing years. Beautiful silver is not only a material possession but also a cultural asset. It becomes a heritage for future generations. Vermeil, which is gilded silver, naturally goes well with china that has gold decoration and where gold suits the dining room.

There is no Sheffield plate made today. It was manufactured for about a hundred years in Sheffield, England, from 1742 to 1840; now it has been replaced by electroplate, which is much less expensive. Before electroplate only the wealthy could afford table silverware. Genuine Sheffield today is valued by collectors as an antique. It is prized particularly for the subtle tones of copper appearing through the silver.

Today, silverplate consists of a base metal coated with a layer of pure silver by the process of electroplating. The base metal used by most silverware manufacturers today is known as 18 per cent nickel silver. It is composed of about 65 per cent copper, 17 per cent zinc, and 18 per cent nickel. Silver used for plating is 99.9 per cent pure. The main difference between inferior and fine silverplate is the amount of silver used in the plating.

Dirilyte, an alloy of different metals, is another tableware chosen when gold is preferred to silver. Its finish and color are permanent. It is solid and unplated, and the knife blades can be sharpened.

Stainless steel has become popular over the last decade or so, for casual living. Steel knife blades for silverware have been made successfully since the early 1930s, but the formula for this type of stainless steel could not be adapted to pattern molding. After World War II, the processing methods were finally developed which made possible in the late 1950s the production of stainless steel shapes interesting in design and of varying thickness, weight, and balance.

LEFT: The coin-silver tea and coffee service on the buffet was made by Charles A. Burnett in America in 1804.

OPPOSITE: A table or buffet set with handsome silver has an undeniable elegance, and at one time a man's financial worth was judged by his collection. Pickard's china pattern "Savannah" with its wreath of ivy leaves seemed appropriate for this Christmas table.

STORING AND CARE OF FLATWARE

Constant use enhances the beauty of sterling; the minute network of tiny scratches developed over years of use forms the patina of unsurpassed richness seen on rare silver in museums. However, it should not be scratched deliberately or by tumbling it around in a dishpan or dishwasher. If its use is rotated so that all pieces get equal treatment, it will rarely tarnish. Sterling should be washed immediately after use in hot soapy water, then rinsed thoroughly and dried carefully with a soft cloth. Do not let silverware drain dry and never leave it dirty overnight. Salt and fatty foods left on it for any length of time can

LEFT: A five-piece place setting for luncheon, with the salad fork outside and the butter knife on top of the plate. The silverware is "Spring Garden" by Holmes & Edwards. BELOW LEFT: Here the salad fork has been equally correctly placed inside, with the butter knife placed on the bottom of the plate. The design is "May Queen" by Holmes & Edwards. BELOW: A six-piece place setting for luncheon or an informal dinner. The silverware design is "Masterpiece" by International Silver Company.

cause pits that are almost impossible to remove. Polish silver occasionally with a liquid or cream polish specially prepared for the purpose. Use a small soft brush for the crevices in ornamental silver. After a long period of disuse silver will tarnish until it is almost black and must then be given a more thorough cleaning in this manner. Cleaning silver seems to be a bugbear — I do not know why, for everything has to be cleaned in one way or another, and gleaming silver is so rewarding. Sulphur, salt, and acid are the primary substances responsible for tarnish. Salad dressing, eggs, rubber of all kinds (including the rubber drainboard you may have by your sink and the rubber bands sometimes used to hold a place setting), and even the moisture from your hands, will cause tarnish.

Silver should be stored away from the air in a clean, dry place, either in flannel rolls, a chest lined with tarnish-preventing cloth, or in a similarly treated buffet drawer. Zipper-closing bags are excellent for large pieces. Silverplate requires the same care as sterling.

Finally, when acquiring silver, buy the best you can afford from the most knowledgeable and reputable dealer in your vicinity, and listen to his advice. Take plenty of time to

LEFT: Formal dinner setting with seven pieces of flatware. BELOW: Wedding buffet showing a cake sword. All the silver is by Reed & Barton.

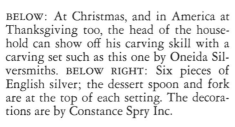

BELOW: At Christmas, and in America at Thanksgiving too, the head of the household can show off his carving skill with a carving set such as this one by Oneida Silversmiths. BELOW RIGHT: Six pieces of English silver; the dessert spoon and fork are at the top of each setting. The decorations are by Constance Spry Inc.

ABOVE: The arrangement of flatware at a buffet is for convenience as well as effect. A simple solution for an informal buffet is shown here with the utensils placed on the napkin.

ABOVE: The Georg Jensen company, founded in Denmark in 1904, is a famous maker of contemporary sterling silver. The classical design shown here is Jensen's "Acorn" pattern.

RIGHT: A well-balanced buffet arrangement with the knives and forks grouped separately between the folded napkins.

BELOW: A more formal table for eight with the silver grouped on either side of the dinner plates.

decide on your manufacturer and pattern, for it is the beginning of your table plan and should give you pleasure for many years to come. I say "beginning" advisedly, because most people find it easier to choose their silver pattern first, and then their china and glass. Of course, if you are lucky enough to inherit some fine china, you will have more time for the selection of your silver and other accouterments to complement your inheritance.

The following is a list of the most commonly used flatware and holloware (see Chapter 11).

FLATWARE

LARGE FORK. Usually called a dinner fork although it is used for lunch and dinner when meat is served. Also used with tablespoon for serving.

LARGE KNIFE. Companion piece to large fork.

SMALLER FORK AND KNIFE. Used for breakfast, lunch, and dinner, except for the meat course. This fork may be used for dessert, and, with a dessert spoon, is more commonly used in England than in America. It may be used for salad, and in some services it is made specially for this course. This size of fork and knife is used for the fish course when there are no fish knives and forks.

FISH KNIFE AND FORK. Used mostly in Europe and from old services. Americans use the small fork and knife for fish today.

SOUPSPOON. Used for all soups, desserts, cereal, and ice cream. The round bowl is most commonly used here in America, the egg-shaped bowl in Europe. It is between the teaspoon and the tablespoon in size. Both shapes may used as small serving pieces.

TEASPOON. Used for tea, regular coffee cups, fruit and dessert in sherbet glasses, and for grapefruit (unless you have the pointed spoon specially designed for this fruit).

COFFEE SPOON. Used for small, after-dinner coffee service, and as a baby's feeding spoon.

DESSERT SPOON. Used with the small fork for dessert. Also used for soup and cereal.

TABLESPOON. Used mainly for serving vegetables, salads, berries, fruits, and desserts.

INDIVIDUAL SALAD FORK. Used for salad, pies, and pastries. American designs have one wide tine for cutting greens.

BUTTER KNIFE. For individual use on the bread-and-butter plate for butter, jam and jellies, etc. Also for hors d'oeuvres and cheeses.

OYSTER FORK. Small three-pronged fork designed for eating oysters, clams, or any cold shellfish cocktail.

FRUIT KNIFE AND FORK. Mostly used in Europe when serving fruit at the end of a meal.

ICED-BEVERAGE SPOON. With its long slender handle it is needed for iced tea, iced coffee, fruit drinks, milk shakes, and parfaits. It is also used for mixing highballs.

The dessert and fruit course can be a glamorous finale, with a setting of beautiful silver and glass. Here the dessert silver is placed above the china, in the English fashion. The glass is Early American and English cranberry, with the water glasses standing in ornate Persian silver holders. The chair at the far end of the table has a Chinese chairback pad.

The qualities of silver are displayed to advantage in a buffet setting. The arrangement of dried flowers includes delphinium florets, larkspur, blue salvia, celosia, verbena, roses, pom-pom dahlias, feverfew, straw flowers, and ageratum. The foliage is leather-leaf fern, santolina, and ivy. Flower foliage seldom survives the drying process, and unless special hardy foliage is dried separately to add grays and greens to a bouquet, the flowers have to be massed together.

SALT SPOON. The tiniest spoon made, for open salt cellars on formal tables.

LADLES. In various sizes for soup, gravy, sauces, and punch.

CARVING SETS. Large for roast meats, smaller for steaks.

SALAD SET. Salad-bowl servers.

OTHERS: Asparagus tongs
           Sugar and ice tongs
           Lemon or pickle fork
           Sugar spoon
           Pierced vegetable spoon
           Butter-serving knife
           Cold-meat fork
           Pie- or cake-serving knife
           Cheese-serving knife
           Relish spoon — pierced or plain
           Game scissors

HOLLOWARE

VEGETABLE DISH. Perhaps a matching pair, a double dish, or a two-section dish.

OVAL PLATTER. Well-and-tree design.

ROUND PLATTER. The chop size is excellent for serving desserts, cake, aspic, etc.

TRAYS. In various sizes.

CANDLESTICKS AND CANDELABRA.

SALT AND PEPPER SHAKERS, OPEN SALT DISHES.

TEA AND COFFEE SERVICE.

SILVER BOWL. Useful for fruit, flowers, and salad.

COMPOTE. For fruit, nuts, and candies.

PITCHER. For water and other beverages.

BREAD TRAY.

COVERED BUTTER DISH.

GRAVY SET.

WINE COOLER.

CHAFING DISH AND TRAY.

Silver design was greatly affected by the eighteenth-century discovery of plates and cups of silver at Herculaneum such as these, which were buried in A.D. 79.

8.
Glassware

Many things make a table setting attractive and charming but none, except perhaps silver, gives it more sparkle or twinkle than polished glass. The minute the glasses are placed in position, the place setting becomes alive and more elegant. In addition, the height of the glasses adds another dimension. Theirs is the magic in hospitality, for glass captures the light — from the sun, the moon, the chandelier, or the candelabra — and spreads it merrily over the table. This coruscation gives a happy touch that adds to the mood of the festivity.

Sparkling glasses add to the pleasure of drinking anything — and especially wine, for in fine glasses the glowing color of a red wine or the golden bubbles of a champagne shine through. The pleasure of wine becomes more sensuous with fragile hand-blown glasses that barely touch the lips; one without the other is not a true experience. Many famous wine districts have developed their special regional glasses to satisfy every aesthetic sense.

The selection of the "correct" glass to enhance the looks and taste of a drink is as important as the pleasure of "marrying" the wine to the food. A liqueur would lose more than half its pleasure if it were drunk from an earthenware mug. Wine is most enjoyable in a stemmed glass of fine, clear, transparent crystal. Colored or tinted glasses are generally excluded by experts, for they do not do justice to the color of the wine itself, which should be clearly and invitingly displayed. Cut glass, decorated glass, or thick heavy crystal are eliminated for the same reason. These are better reserved for water. They would not, in any case, do for brandy, which requires a glass that can conduct the heat of the hand in order to release the bouquet. Here the bowl should be sufficiently large and of a design, preferably tulip-shaped, to allow air space within the glass where the aroma and bouquet may be enjoyed to their fullest. The short stem of a brandy glass is for general appearance and to enable the hand to cup the bowl. Conversely, the longer stem of the wine glass pre-

OPPOSITE: An engraving of 1875 shows runners bringing the molten glass to the blowers.

vents the hand from warming the wine and thus changing the proper temperature. Today there are many factories which make an all-purpose glass that meets these requirements and is large enough to receive an ample serving, while still being less than half filled. But there is nothing better than the glass that is specially designed for a single purpose.

Champagne glasses, once tall and just wide enough at the top for the bubbles to form, changed to the saucer shape with the hollow stem, which became popular everywhere. The hollow stem, considered unsanitary, has become solid, but these saucer-shaped glasses, hollow stemmed or otherwise, are still thought of as the only ones to associate with champagnes. Experts, however, still decree that the logical shape to enhance this great wine properly is the elongated one on a tall stem. Both shapes are on the market and time will tell which the public finally prefers.

The usual custom for formal dinners is to have all the glassware matching. For private dinners and less formal affairs many hostesses like to mix what they have for the sake of variety. The differing shapes and sizes usually have been selected and purchased to harmonize. Colored glass in many forms has its own brilliant and lively charm. Many people like water glasses in color to liven up their table settings and to tie in with their color schemes. A cut crystal or an etched goblet for water is often used with a plain, clear one for the wine. There is a glass specially made for everything we drink. The variety of shapes and sizes is often confusing to the young housewife, but for the basic table setting three glasses are all that are ever really needed these days, even for the most formal kind of dinner. A banqueting table may sometimes show four — and you will see some photographs in this book, showing a barrage of glasses. But for all practical — and enjoyable — purposes three are enough.

For family and informal meals a water glass (a plain or footed tumbler or a stemmed goblet), a juice glass, and a sherbet glass make a good beginning. A stemmed glass is more interesting, usually more fragile, and therefore more elegant, but much depends on your setting — or preference. To this selection you may want to add iced tea or highball glasses, finger bowls, and punch cups. For the bar you will need, besides the highball glasses, old fashioned V-shaped cocktail glasses and tulip-shaped sherry glasses. You may also add whisky sour, cordial, and brandy glasses if your needs in this direction so dictate. Wine glasses may be chosen from nine basic shapes, but it is usual to be satisfied with two — one for red wine and one for white — in addition to the champagne and sherry glasses already mentioned.

GLASS PLACEMENT

The water glass, in America, goes on every table and is placed just above the tip of the first knife, on the inside. The second glass, no matter what it contains, is placed to the right of the water glass and a little toward the table edge. When a third glass is added — usually at a formal dinner — the second glass is moved back and the third glass (the first to be used) is in the forward position. The glasses now form a triangle.

For informal dinners a sherry or white wine is usually served but, of course, this is a question of personal taste. Formal dinners might also add a sweet wine or champagne with the dessert. The glass for this may be added to the group, or, to avoid a crowded appearance, brought in with the dessert service. Like everything else in table setting, the plan is based on thoughtful consideration of those participating in the meal and a desire to make the place setting and the whole table attractive to the eye, as well as practical. If you prefer to put the glasses in a straight row from the water glass toward the edge of the table, that is your prerogative. In Paris and many other European cities the glasses are placed along the top of the place setting in a group or a row (see Chapter 11).

Glass in every conceivable form, texture, and quality is so easily available to us today that we take the wide choice for granted. However, because there is such a wide choice, it is helpful to know certain facts about glass before beginning a collection that one hopes will remain for many years to come.

A most interesting experience is a visit to a glass factory, especially one where it is possible to watch a practiced artisan take the molten glass and blow, cut, and shape a goblet. Glass-blowers move with the rhythm and coordination of a dancer, and one senses the years of training when they work with such precision. Indeed, in glass-blowing, the seconds count. To observe a talent that can so quickly produce a work of great beauty is fascinating; at the same time it gives one not only a proper respect for the art of glassmaking, but a greater interest in choosing glassware of high quality. Each shape has been most carefully designed — and tested — for the drinker's maximum enjoyment. Experimentation proves this to be true.

GLASS TERMS

Crystal glass was so named because the first efforts at making it were an attempt to copy rock crystal. "Crystal" means clear and transparent, but all the clear glass we see is not necessarily crystal. True crystal has a high percentage of lead and gives a clear ringing tone when tapped. Its high luster and ability to refract light make it ideal for cutting and engraving. It is also known as "flint glass" and "lead glass." The first man to perfect lead crystal was George Ravenscroft, a seventeenth-century Englishman. Stemmed crystal goblets are the most exquisite acquisition for any formal table setting — and they are likely to surprise you with their strength and durability.

Hand-blown glass stemware is literally blown into shape by a "gatherer," with a four-foot pipe. The process is almost faster than the eye can perceive — that is, until one has seen it happen several times. Because these glasses are fashioned by hand they often contain slight irregularities. These so-called personality traits can be endearing, and they stamp the article as being hand-made.

Hand-pressed glassware is heavier than hand-blown glass. It is formed in a carefully designed, hand-sculptured mold which gives it not only its shape, but its ornamentation as well. This process, perfected in America in the 1820s, reduced the price of glass and made it available at little cost to us today. Many collectors find that the early pieces make valuable additions to their table settings.

Cut glass is decorated by cutting patterns or figures into the surface. Antique shops are filled with nineteenth-century cut-glass bowls, compotes, vases, and goblets. These are typical of a grandmother's collection and of the day when they served as popular wedding presents.

Etched glass has designs that are more intricate but less deep than are found in cut glass. The glass is coated with wax, then the design or pattern is scratched through the wax to the glass surface. The glass is next dipped into a bath of acid which eats only into the exposed areas or lines on the surface. In other words, the wax resists the acid.

Other types of glass that are collected are lead glass, lime glass, cased glass, overlay glass, and milk glass. Space does not permit detailed descriptions of all these types, but they can be found listed in specialized books such as *5000 Years of Glass*, written in 1954 by a Czechoslovakian, Jaroslav R. Vavra.

HISTORICAL SURVEY

Glass was used for beads and ceramic glazing in Mesopotamia about 3500 B.C., and the Egyptians made or imported glass vases four thousand years ago. The Romans enjoyed it in many forms in their villas. Pieces of glass still exist that were made before the Christian era. Then the blowing tube had been invented and most of the techniques used today were already known. Although there have been certain refinements, the basic technique for blown glass has remained the same for the last two thousand years.

During the Roman conquest glassmaking developed in both quality and quantity, and later spread to France, Germany, Spain, and England. The practice of it also spread eastward to Asia. Unlike silver, glass was a cheap commodity, available to both the rich and the poor; consequently its development and use was on a much broader scale.

The Italians were the first to create an actual style in glassmaking. During the eleventh century, the northward development centered in and around Venice and by the end of the thirteenth century the island of Murano was the home of the best glass. "Venetian" glass has been renowned ever since, and rarely does a visitor to that remarkable city return home without at least one piece of it as a souvenir. Artistically, the present-day Venetian glass varies greatly, but superb glassware is still made, along with the tourist items. In the

Drinking vessels made during the years 1750-1835. From left to right: an engraved rummer, a punch cup, a champagne flute, a wine glass with molded bowl, a wine glass with air twist stem, a tavern "dram," a wine glass with engraved bowl, and an ale glass.

fifteenth century the Venetians discovered soda-lime glass and called it "cristallo." The prestige that followed in the sixteenth century was such that their delicate glass goblets became famous throughout civilized Europe. These goblets were probably the first glass ones to replace the traditional silver and gold vessels used for the drinking of wine. This commercial monopoly created the same situation that later developed at Meissen. Jealousy and fear of losing their reputation made the Venetians impose strict regulations to safeguard their secrets. But notwithstanding the threats of dire penalties, the workmen succeeded in escaping to Germany, Bohemia, Holland, and England, and they took with them the knowledge and ability that ended in the founding of many rival factories.

In 1676 George Ravenscroft developed a formula for making lead glass or flint glass which lent itself to cutting and engraving. It was much clearer than the Venetian soda glass, and its development put an end to British imports from Venice. From then on, until the nineteenth century, England remained ahead in glass manufacture. Because the soda glass cooled quickly the Venetians were able to produce the rapid twists and turns that characterize their work. English lead crystal, on the other hand, cooled more slowly, allowing a longer working period for the development of the design and for making gentler curves. By the eighteenth century glassware had improved greatly in quality, keeping pace with china and silver, so this became a very rich era in the history of table setting. Production increased for all types of drinking glasses, including wine glasses with an air twist in the stem. In the latter, the air was entrapped to become an integral part of the design.

In the seventeenth and eighteenth centuries, glass table accessories included various receptacles for ice in water. The lumps of ice and ice water were used to cool the mouth after eating the heavily spiced, fiery sauces that were served with the fashionable dried and salted foods of the day. Dining rooms often became sultry from the heat of braziers of red-hot charcoal; wine was preferred as cold as possible and thus the monteith came into use. This vessel, with its scalloped edge, is not a punch bowl, as some collectors think; the U-shaped depressions in the rim held the wineglass stem while the wineglass bowl was washed or cooled in the iced water. Later, individual wineglass coolers were placed to the right of each person.

The first monteiths were made of various metals (silver, gold, pewter, and copper), then of delftware, flint glass, porcelain, and creamware. The individual one- and two-lipped wineglass coolers were made of glass and were accompanied by glass water plates. They were also called water-glasses. Understandably, this duplication of names caused much confusion in advertisements that listed "water-glasses" with drinking vessels and tumbler-like glasses that were meant only for rinsing the mouth at table. These tumblers, which were quite different in shape from the water-glasses, were the predecessors of our finger bowls. Glass finger bowls, also called finger cups, date no earlier than 1760.

Handsome table services of deeply cut flint glass, consisting of two hundred to five hundred matching pieces — combining dessert and wine service — were made during the Regency and George IV periods. Wineglass coolers and finger bowls were included in these handsome collections. Tumblers — named because their wide base prevented them from tipping over when they were used in swaying coaches — were first made in silver and enclosed in a leather case. Later they were made of glass in quarter-, half-, and full-pint sizes and were used for drinking beer, claret, and sack. Pressed tumblers were made in America about 1840, and as they became increasingly available to a wide public they ended up by being used for the drinking of water too.

The introduction of machines that blow and press glass has satisfied a large mass market. However, the art of glass-blowing by mouth is still producing large quantities of beautiful table glass that remains much in demand today.

On page 148 is Irish glass from the distinguished factory at Waterford, where every piece is hand-blown and hand-cut, just as it first was almost two hundred years ago. Waterford is treasured for its blue tint or "soapy" appearance.

The European glass industry boasts many famous factories, among them Baccarat, a long-honored name in crystal throughout the world. Now two hundred years old, the Baccarat enterprise still resides in a small town in Lorraine about 250 miles east of Paris. In 1816 Baccarat began to concentrate on the production of full-lead crystal and has done so ever since. Opposite are the cut-crystal glasses shown at an exhibition in 1878, and on page 131 is an example of their modern stemware "Saint Exupéry." I made these table settings in 1966 at their Paris showrooms. Lalique, another French glass known for its delicacy, is represented on page 130.

Orrefors glass, which has also been manufactured for more than two hundred years,

LEFT: The old French custom of placing stemware at the top of the place setting and turning the fork tines and the soup spoon down is still followed. These five shapes in cut crystal goblets were made by Baccarat in 1878. Typically French are the saucer-shaped champagne glass and the glass knife rest.
BELOW: A state dinner set for Queen Elizabeth II at the Louvre, Paris, showing Baccarat glasses set in the same way.

BELOW: English compote with cover and stand, decorated with copperwheel engraving, mid-eighteenth century.

ABOVE: Setting for the first course in an informal dinner. The English crystal is Stuart's "Aragon" pattern, with Royal Worcester's "Malvern" china and Worcester's silver flatware.

LEFT: Austrian crystal wine and water goblets are used here with clear crystal stemware. Hurricane glasses give height to the settings without obstruction.

OPPOSITE: A table set entirely with glass pieces, all of which were hand made by master craftsmen of Corning Glass.

LEFT: In English-speaking countries the tumbler or stemmed water goblet is placed above the tip of the first knife.

LEFT: When two glasses, for water and wine, are used, the second glass is placed to the right of the water glass and slightly toward the diner. ABOVE: A third glass takes the place of the second in the forward position, as it is the first to be used, and the second moves back, thus forming a triangle. The goblets are Lalique.

ABOVE: A setting for a state dinner in honor of Queen Frederika of Greece at the Colony Restaurant, New York City. In the United States the fourth glass for a sweet wine or champagne (in position here next to the water glass) is often brought in with the dessert service to avoid a cluttered table, except at large formal dinners and banquets. BELOW: Modern Baccarat stemware, including the flute champagne glass, set across the top of the place setting.

is the outstanding Swedish make. On page 70 some of this glass is to be seen in a place setting created in Stockholm.

The green glass of Germany is used on page 260, where the color plays such an important part in the over-all effect of the setting.

Among the least expensive, but by no means the least attractive, glass is that made in Mexico. Mexican glass tumblers with their characteristic irregular form are delightful for children's tables, as on page 247.

Owing to the stringent migration laws governing glassworkers, the United States was handicapped in the development of its glass industry. British legislation forced the colonies to import glass from England and Ireland. The first attempt at making glass in the United States was in 1608, but the seventeenth century was almost glassless. However, much was learned from immigrant craftsmen, and in 1739 a glass factory was set up in New Jersey, to be followed by others in New York and New England. All this glass had the same general characteristics and is classified as the "South Jersey" type. Later, from 1769 to 1774, Stiegel produced some glass for the table. However, in 1772, a wide variety of tablewares was apparently manufactured at Philadelphia by the brothers Elliott. Forty attempts were made to establish glass factories in New England, but most of these failed after the War of 1812. The two most successful survivors, the New England Glass Company and the Boston & Sandwich Glass Company, finally gave way to competition from Midwestern factories, located where coal and natural gas were abundant. The glassware made by New Englanders did not compare with English and Irish imports, but at the beginning of the nineteenth century their invention of pressed glass was one of the few technical innovations since the first attempts at glass-blowing. This mechanical substitute for cut glass became a household commodity around 1845. These New England factories achieved great variety of form and excellent texture, and their organization and standardization probably set the pattern for the successful modern factories.

It is hard to determine exactly when a glass was made specifically for drinking water. Goblets, wine glasses, and tumblers were certainly available for a variety of beverages but were seldom used for water. On early American tables wine glasses and tumblers were used for cider and wine, the popular drinks. After the temperance movement spread, they may have been used for water, until Corning made glasses especially for this purpose at its Somerville, Massachusetts, factory in 1851.

The achievements of the Corning Glass Works and Steuben of Corning, New York, are known the world over. The major exhibitions both in America and in Europe are testimony to their unique position in the modern world of glass. The state of Ohio has its share of fine glass factories too: the Libbey Company of Toledo, Heisey of Newark, and Fostoria, in the town of the same name.

For informal meals a mixture of glassware that harmonizes with the setting has become fashionable, such as the milk-glass goblets combined here with clear glass. The ceramic roosters are from Portugal.

THE CARE OF GLASSWARE

The fragile appearance of glass makes many people nervous about handling it, but most glass is stronger than one might think. It is nervous fingers that let it slip, so glass should be grasped firmly while cleaning it.

To keep glassware glistening, wash it in warm, soapy water and dry it while still damp, with a lint-free towel. Care should be taken not to expose fine table glass to extremes in temperature and never store it upside down, because the rim is the most vulnerable part.

Roman mosaic, second century A.D.

9.

Decorations and Centerpieces

If cookery is an art you have mastered, you probably set a beautiful table too. Following an exact recipe in cooking is relatively simple, but we all know that great cooks add their own pinch of "this and that." Setting down rules for decorating a table when the actual ingredients are continually changing is obviously impossible. There are, however, certain principles and procedures which should be adhered to if the results are to be the best that are possible. Decorating, after all, always has been and always will be a question of personal taste and ability. Yet, with a simple approach and an open mind, even those who say they have no ability but who are keenly interested can develop charming tables that will lead them on to creating the most surprising and delightful arrangements.

Many of the settings shown here look time-consuming, and you may favor only the quick and easy to do. But I believe that the more time given to something worth while, the greater the return. It is a good rule, however, to attempt at first only that which you have the time and inclination to finish. For instance, on page 97 the table decoration is a wire lettuce basket filled with shiny green apples. This example may not be appropriate with your particular setting, but it does show how a pretty table can be decorated with simplicity in a few minutes. Furthermore, this idea may be adapted by using red apples or peppers, oranges or lemons — or some other fruit or vegetable that has just the color you want. And the lettuce basket may be changed for another container more suited to your table.

A circular Victorian posy is a quick and easy way to arrange flowers. To make one, fill a shallow bowl with an outer circle of ivy leaves (or galax leaves from the florist, or parsley from the vegetable market). Next, arrange a solid circle of round flowers (asters, carnations, petunias, zinnias, etc.) harmonizing in shape and color. Add a frothy circle of gypsophila (dried or fresh) or small bunches of some other dainty flower to create a contrast. Then fill in the center with a rose and a few of its leaves.

The idea of cut flowers in water for indoor decorating does not go back further than the early nineteenth century, although loose blossoms have been scattered around, especially on dining-room tables, from time immemorial, as much for their perfume as for their color and form.

In the eighteenth century, farmers in New England placed a large charger (today we sometimes use a handsome covered tureen) in the center of the table, from which everyone served himself. Later perhaps this might have been a bowl holding fruit. Both were placed on the bare table for daily family fare. Fresh table linen was kept for guests and special occasions. The squire's family in the village and people with fine homes in Boston "set out" or "covered" their tables with dishes that were placed in a balanced and well-planned manner, and depended on the effect of the garnished food and crisp linen for a pleasing appearance. These tables were somewhat similar in appearance to our present-day buffets.

A horsehoe-shaped banquet table for dessert, planned in Spain, c. 1747, has a central fountain which was used for milk, wine, or water. There are gardens (2), pavilions (3), baskets containing pyramids of sweets (4), and dishes of iced wafers, biscuits, cheeses, and fruit.

On eighteenth-century English tables, according to one of Horace Walpole's essays, written in 1753,

> jellies, biscuits, sugar-plums, and creams have long given way to harlequins, gondoliers, Turks, Chinese and shepherdesses of Saxon china. But these, unconnected, and only seeming to wander among groves of curled paper and silk flowers, were soon discovered to be too insipid and unmeaning. By degrees whole meadows of cattle of the same brittle materials, spread themselves

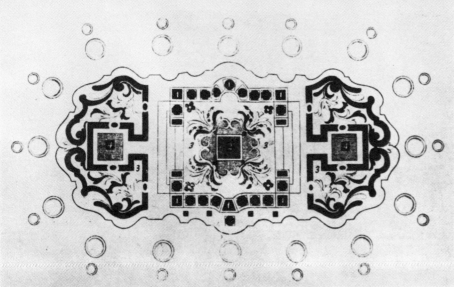

ABOVE: "The Reform Banquet," painted by an English artist in 1832, shows the great emphasis that was being given to decorating the table. LEFT: An eighteenth-century French centerpiece seen from the side and from above. At the center of the square formed by the balustrade (1) was a pedestal (2), and in the flower beds were symbolic figures (4).

over the whole table; cottages rose in sugar, and temples in barley sugar; pigmy Neptunes in cars of cockle-shells triumphed over oceans of looking-glass or seas of silver tissue and at length the whole system of Ovid's [a famous confectioner] and other great professors had been introduced into the science of hieroglyphic eating.

Later, in England, the potted palm and fern were strongly advocated for everyday

LEFT: The White House table in 1899, with a central hedge of greenery. Smilax and asparagus fern are draped everywhere and potted palms are lavishly used. BELOW: The state dining table in the White House, 1902. Huge groups of plants dominate the table.

A table set in London for a diplomatic dinner at the beginning of the twentieth century. The tall arrangement of Wichuriana roses in the center was called an "Ellen Terry" stand. This was a period of lavish center decorations, with garlands separating each place setting. A dining room without potted palms on pedestals would have been thought naked.

use, and only hothouse flowers were thought elegant enough to grace formal tables for social events. Above right is a picture of a banquet table, set in 1832, with pyramids of plant material and dishes of fruit. This was also the era for smilax and asparagus fern, which were draped everywhere. In 1895, a penny-weekly magazine published in England stated that "...the two circles are lengths of the lovely green climber, smilax, without which table decorations would be quite at sea."

At the beginning of the twentieth century, however, any restraint seemed to fly to the winds as the abundance of everything on the tables became awesome. The tables at the White House literally groaned. In fact, the pictures on page 137 make one wonder how it was possible to see that there were other guests sitting on the other side of the hedge of greenery. Then a decade later huge groups of plants dominated both the table and the room in a fashion we would find overpowering today.

Formal English tables also displayed high standards of baskets loaded and dripping with flowers. The center of the table was completely covered with banks of the same flowers, and garlands of green led out to the very edge of the table, separating each place setting. Old English books tell of "colourful lavishness," and their "floral etiquette" was strongly stated and taken with great seriousness.

Today the interest in setting a pretty table has spread far beyond the banquet hall and the fashionable dinner. Luncheons, cocktails, buffets, and suppers, as well as dinners, are occasions that claim attention, as does every other aspect of keeping an attractive, well-run house.

138

Probably the single most variable element in a table arrangement is the centerpiece. For formal tables the centerpiece is placed in the center, for a well-balanced effect. However, it is often the fashion to place a decoration at either end of the table, or, when the setting is on only one side of the table, to place it toward the back. When a circular table is set for three people, a convenient place for the decoration is where the fourth setting would have been. And so the placement of any decoration really becomes a question of convenience, suitability, and balance.

More rigid is the requirement that whatever the centerpiece, it should not be so large that it prevents one person from conversing easily with another across the table. Buffet arrangements, of course, are another matter.

A centerpiece is usually made to stand higher than the more functional elements of the table, thereby relieving the generally flat appearance of the setting as a whole. Either

"La desserte," by Henri Matisse, 1897. Compotes of fruit and a central epergne of fruit and flowers are a practical French way to decorate a dining table.

Exquisite pieces such as the two pictured here are rare, but there are many decorative pieces of ceramics available for table decoration. ABOVE: A Meissen potpourri vase, c. 1747. LEFT: "The Music Lesson," copied from François Boucher's *"L'Agréable Leçon,"* made of Chelsea porcelain, c. 1765. OPPOSITE: In winter, dried bouquets are a great boon to the hostess. This enchanting centerpiece contains feverfew, larkspur, roses, pom-pom dahlias, blue salvia. tamarisk, and santolina foliage, all picked at the height of their bloom and dried in a dark attic. The china is Royal Worcester's "Florizel" pattern.

in color or in form, it should be so related to these other elements that the theme of the table plan is attractively carried out.

Many people create a centerpiece that can remain as a more or less permanent fixture. For this they carefully select an object or material which in color and texture is in character with the room and tableware. This might well be porcelain figurines or ceramics, as shown on this page, or an arrangement of dried flowers (see opposite), which is equally suitable for the winter season or for dry, hot apartment houses. One of the most practical centerpieces is a bowl of fresh fruit which can be enjoyed as dessert and easily replaced. Galax and ivy leaves placed between the fruit separate the form and color and make the arrangement more attractive. Special festive occasions call for many different materials and for ideas that depend on the ability and taste of the hostess. Fresh flowers are of course the general favorite, and I think this will always be so.

LEFT: Table centerpieces should be low enough to allow easy across-the-table conversation. However, a taller arrangement of lacy flowers like this airy bouquet of Australian wild flowers need not be an obstruction. CENTER: An arrangement of waxed flowers and

You may, like myself, use all these decorations at different times to make a happy change. But whatever decorative material is used, it should always be selected to enhance the table as a whole and make a satisfactory picture in the room itself. While following the principles of good design, you should take care that the centerpiece is appropriate to the theme of the occasion and is not distracting or overpowering in any manner.

Fresh flowers are selected for several reasons, but primarily because they add that touch of life so important with inanimate things. I choose my flowers for variety of color and form, and I like to play one against the other. Should all the flowers be small, then it is best to group them and not place tiny dots of color all around, as this usually results in a spotty "pin-cushion" effect, attracting the eye in every direction at once. I find excitement in simplicity, and great satisfaction in achieving the kind of harmony in a flower arrangement that we find in nature itself. Rarely does a so-called stylized bouquet give the pleasure that a natural-looking one gives, where the arranger has obviously understood the quality and nature of her material. Each flower has a certain personality, and to try to mix elegant, formal types like clematis with the coarser and bolder-looking forms and colors of marigolds, for instance, is to give neither of them a fair chance to look at its best on the table.

Everyone has his favorite kind of flower, just as one has favorite styles of furniture and color schemes. Variations of white or yellow flowers with complementary foliage have always given me great pleasure on the table, and here, when the colors are so closely related,

142

fruits combined with fresh foliage makes a long-lasting arrangement. RIGHT: A table centerpiece of handmade flowers by Constance Spry. The table is covered with a heavy-weight cotton cloth, and Wedgwood earthenware is set on straw leaf fans for a unique effect.

it is easy to mix a variety of form and texture. White and soft yellow together are also always enjoyable and appropriate in the majority of settings. If the arrangement is set directly on highly polished dark wood, the reflection can add to the over-all charm.

Lavender and blue flowers look better in the daytime than under artificial light and are therefore a better choice for a luncheon than for an evening dinner or buffet. Vibrant reds and oranges have a rich and demanding quality, and are a good choice where warmth and dramatic effects are desired. Their colors react well under electric or candle light.

FOLIAGE AND DRIED FLOWERS

As in nature, green is a good foil for all colors and looks attractive in every setting. Arranging interesting foliage with good form may represent a challenge, but it makes a most satisfactory bouquet in the hot summer, and the fact that foliage will outlast most flowers makes it very well worth while attempting. The mixture of shiny leaves like laurel or camellia with sprays of broom, or long needled pine and the swordlike foliage of gladioli or iris, can produce interesting contrasts in texture and form.

Garlands and wreaths demand more professional skill, but if you have a mind and a hand for them and use appropriate material they will last for many parties and family affairs at the holiday seasons.

In wintertime, dried flowers and ferns are a great boon, especially for those without a garden. A certain amount of patience and time is required for drying them. My own schedule limits me to ferns which I gather in July and place between newspaper under a heavy carpet, ready to use for fall arrangements. Flowers can also be dried by hanging them in a dark and dry place, like an attic. They should always be picked at the height of their bloom. Among the most suited to drying are celosia, yarrow, gypsophila, helichrysum, statice, larkspur, hydrangea, cornflower, aster, etc.

Fresh flowers and vines may be added to enliven fruit, vegetable, and dried combinations, if the stems are inserted in plastic water picks. These picks, available at florists', are easily hidden from view.

CONTAINERS

Most important to the centerpiece decoration is the selection of a suitable container. I restrict myself to shapes that are appropriate to the form and period of my tables and to the kind of plant material I enjoy arranging most. Nontransparent vessels are, on the whole, easiest to manage, but several glass goblets are useful for certain types of decorations. The problem with using glass is to conceal the stems and holder or to make the stems count as part of the design. If you can spare them, vegetable dishes that match your china service make perfect centerpiece containers. Throughout the book are illustrations of decorations made in containers of other materials and of various shapes. Most of these were selected for special events or because they were available and appropriate for the particular setting.

A PRACTICAL APPROACH TO FLOWER CENTERPIECES

If you have a garden, select and cut the flowers the day before you intend to arrange them. Use a sharp knife or proper garden secateurs. Remove at least one-third of the foliage from the bottom of the stem as well as all imperfect growth. Choose a cool place and let the stems soak in deep water overnight so they will harden. It hardly need be said that a wilted — or wilting — bouquet has a depressing effect on everyone.

If you buy flowers from a florist, place your order when your party plans are complete, for some flowers — perhaps those you most wanted — are not in stock every day. Have them delivered early enough so that you can recut the stems and soak them for two hours in deep water. In addition, allow plenty of time for unhurried attention when you are ready to do the arranging.

It is easier, faster, and more enjoyable if you have convenient space near your water supply and have the container, holder, and everything else you may need in readiness.

You will have your own favorite flower holders. Some people use pin or needle holders almost exclusively, but I have never found anything better than ordinary soft two-inch-mesh chicken wire (wire mesh), sometimes in combination with a sharp needle holder. Chicken wire may be held in place with the plastic clips made for this purpose and available through your florist, or it may be tied in with twine like a package, the string cut loose when you are finished. The crossed stems will hold it firmly in place. When the bouquet needs to be high for a buffet and the container is not very deep, I wedge the wire firmly on top of a suitable needle holder and stretch it up pyramid fashion; the two together will hold anything.

The needle holder may be held firmly to the base of the container with florists' clay. Roll the clay into a sausage shape about the thickness of your little finger and press it firmly around the holder, then onto the dry base of the container.

Many people use spongelike Oasis from the florist, and find it simplifies things for them; it is certainly easier on one's hands than chicken wire.

Small posies or groups of leaves can be arranged in the hand and held together with elastic bands. This is true too for thin stems, like grasses, that one wishes to add quickly.

There is obviously more to flower arranging than this, and numerous books have been written by experts demonstrating the countless ways of doing it. However, as a last word of practical advice, let me remind you to keep the water level up and to cut off or remove any wilted leaf or flower so that you may enjoy your bouquets for the longest possible time.

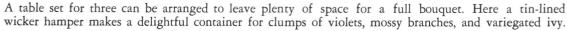

A table set for three can be arranged to leave plenty of space for a full bouquet. Here a tin-lined wicker hamper makes a delightful container for clumps of violets, mossy branches, and variegated ivy.

LEFT: Most wedding receptions take place in restaurants, clubs, or hotels, and the wedding cake is placed on a separate table to await the cutting ceremony. When the reception is held at home the cake can form a centerpiece.

OPPOSITE: For long tables a dual centerpiece can be most effective. Here begonias, roses, fuchsias, carnations, and anemones duplicate the rich colors in the service plates, red wine glasses, and carpet. The early Capo di Monte china and the Venetian stemware are eighteenth-century. The salt holders are by Cellini.

UNUSUAL CENTERPIECES

Some of the illustrations also show centerpieces created of novel materials, such as the flowers made from tin cans for a Mexican setting on page 151, and the blown eggs attached to bare branches with ribbons to make a gay children's Easter table on page 247. Other ideas for unusual centerpieces are: a collection of shells, arranged in a flat oval basket for a table beside a swimming pool, on page 150; artificial arrangements done as tastefully as those originated by Constance Spry (page 143), or made up of tissue paper and foil roses as on page 62; and for those who cannot or will not prune an evergreen—or whose home is too hot for fresh materials to survive at Christmastime—a table decorated with gift packages to be demolished as soon as possible. Such an arrangement, shown on page 153, might be adapted to a birthday or Easter party.

CANDLES

I refer to candles more fully in the next chapter, but should mention here that dinner and supper tables are the only ones that may have the added glamour of candlelight. Most people naturally prefer tall candles so that the flickering light is above eye level, and tall candelabra with many candles add the richness and romance that belong on a special table or buffet. Candlesticks in various heights and periods (preferably of the same material) may be grouped together for light and effect when branch candelabra are not available.

RIGHT: A French country dining table combines elegance with informality. The candelabra and decorated epergne contrast with the simple compotes and the wine bottle.

OPPOSITE: China with rich design can be made even more arresting on the table by a cloth that emphasizes its color. The early Royal Worcester arranged with Waterford glass and English sterling.

10.
Accessories
and Props

The title of this chapter may sound rather theatrical. In fact, when setting a special table, I am inclined to view the whole room as a "set" and to think of the individual decorations (not only of the table but elsewhere in the dining room) as "props." This chapter covers the items that contribute to the setting and strengthen its general theme.

Under "accessories" I include candleholders, salt, pepper, and mustard containers, the old-fashioned cruet stand, decanters, cigarette and match holders, mint and sweetmeat dishes — in fact, everything other than the centerpiece, which has already been discussed, and china, glass, silver, linen, and dishes actually used for food service.

CANDLES AND HOLDERS

Many beautifully designed candlesticks and candelabra have been made in Europe, yet, surprisingly, candles are not used as extensively in England and on the Continent as they are in America. In Europe, candlelight seems to be reserved for special events, for

149

special displays, and for special people, whereas Americans are almost inclined to overdo it by putting candles on every table possible, including afternoon tea tables set for club functions. While photographing tables in France for this book, and also while doing the same in a large city in England, I had found it difficult to find candles of any kind, particularly off-white tapers in the length I wanted. In contrast, the variety of colors and lengths offered in the average American department store and in the packaged candles sold in most food stores and gift shops is very wide.

As every hostess knows (and every female guest appreciates), candlelight is the most flattering light at dinnertime. Although men like to see women look their prettiest, they also want to see what they are eating, so the first requirement is that you have enough candles to light the table properly or have extra light from wall sconces or other fixtures.

The second requirement, also mentioned in the previous chapter, is that all candles be tall enough to be above eye level in order to avoid the often repeated error of having candles flickering in the eyes of guests. Short candles may be placed at either end of the table in lieu of a place setting, to eliminate this problem. For buffets and other tables the candle height should be in proportion to the holder.

The hostess should always have plenty of replacements on hand, for many people do not like to interrupt an interesting conversation to take coffee in the living room, thus breaking the magic circle that sometimes develops around the table. I find I often have to bring in fresh candles with the coffee service.

Whether candles are fat or thin, machine made or hand dipped, dripless, beeswax, twisted, or tapers, all must be firmly fixed in their holders. Rubber candle "grips" to solve this problem are available at many candle counters. Otherwise, florists' clay may be used around the candle base if it is too small to fit the cup firmly. However, perhaps the easiest way of all to make candles fit the holders securely is to put the ends into very hot water for a few seconds until the wax is soft enough to be wedged tightly into the candle cup.

FAR LEFT: Queen Victoria started the vogue for shell work, and many nine-teenth-century pieces are now museum treasures. Small shells are used here for salt. ABOVE: Sunflowers, wall decoration, and candleholders, cut from tin cans, add originality to an informal buffet with earthenware plates, hand-painted in Jamaica. RIGHT: A buffet for men returning from a hunt. BELOW: A dress cloth from Indonesia is a suitable background for brass candlesticks and pottery.

Colored and decorated candles seem to me to be in the category of colored and fancy gloves. Their choice is a matter of taste, to be governed by the formality of the occasion. Red candles are most popular at Christmastime, and pale or muted colors are often useful to emphasize a particular color scheme in informal settings. However, ivory or antique white candles are more appropriate for formal affairs anywhere and look equally well on informal occasions. Branched candelabra seem more formal than candlesticks, and yet in the right setting candlesticks do have their own charm and are perfectly correct to use.

No matter what your holders are made of — silver, pewter, glass, tin, porcelain, pottery, or hand-wrought iron — they are part of the decoration and should be placed to balance the table setting as well as to light it adequately and attractively.

For outdoor tables where candlelight is preferred and, in fact, for all patio and garden lighting (unless you have a way with the weatherman) hurricane covers will be needed. Vigil candles in glass holders and wicks that float on salad oil are delightful alternatives.

SALT AND PEPPER HOLDERS

Silver salt and pepper shakers with matching open salt and mustard dishes are both functional and attractive accessories. However, today pepper grinders are fashionable among epicures who like their pepper freshly ground.

Matching salt and pepper shakers are made of every conceivable material to go with any tableware for any setting. The important consideration is that they be placed for convenience. The correct procedure is to place at least a pair for every two guests on formal occasions and at each end of the table for informal family dining. It is also important to check that they pour freely, for nothing is more embarrassing than to see guests struggling with a clogged salt shaker. This is apt to happen most in the summer, or in humid climates. A good remedy is to place a little rice in the bottom of a salt shaker to absorb the moisture.

OTHER ACCESSORIES

Cigarette holders and matches may be placed at the top of a place setting if individual preferences are known, or set between two persons. Otherwise cigarettes are usually passed when the coffee is served, and not before.

When space allows, compotes or dishes of nuts or sweetmeats such as mints are usually placed on the table. Decanters, holding sufficient wine for the course they are intended for, are placed beside the host for table service, or on the sideboard if a servant is in attendance.

OPPOSITE: Christmas-tree ornaments hung from a chandelier — a good idea when there is no space for a tree. The porcelain dinnerware, crystal, and sterling are by Rosenthal.

PROPS

Props are usually subsidiary to the centerpiece, but sometimes they can be the *raison d'être* of the whole setting. On page 259, for instance, the pewter ducks form the main decoration and the flowers are set apart at the end of the table. The emphasis is a little different on the Easter table on page 247, where the props — the little individual tulip "plants" — sustain the idea of the centerpiece, a bare tree trimmed with blown and decorated eggs.

For weddings and other special occasions — particularly at Christmastime — the decorative theme is extended beyond the dining table. On page 111, for instance, a garland of winter greens decorates the table, and a pair of small cone-shaped trees made up of the same material is used on the buffet or sideboard. In addition, swags or wreaths can decorate a dining-room fireplace — with matching decorations on the wall sconces.

At summer garden parties it is effective to use standing candelabra or torches and decorate them with the same material or motif used on the table. Another way of strengthening the color scheme and extending the "set" is to use miniature fairy lights (saved from Christmas) and twist them around a nearby shrub.

Many households have tall plant stands filled with growing plants. These props can be placed at either side of a doorway or buffet and fresh flowers can be added to the green plants simply by placing the flower stems in plastic water picks and inserting them in the plant pot. You can use the same variety of flower for the dining table. In the same way, a window box of green plants can be brought into the setting by enlivening it with a few fresh flowers in the varieties or colors used elsewhere in the room.

A very different kind of prop is the gun rack on page 151, forming the background for a safari buffet, and unusual, too, is the ornamental stone garden figure seen on page 87.

In Europe it has long been fashionable to set the centerpiece on a glass or mirrored plateau. This prop not only enlarges the centerpiece but serves the practical purpose of preventing any water that may leak over the brim of the container (when this is being refilled) from staining a cloth or marking a table top. In addition, the mirror reflects some of the flowers and adds to the general sparkle and charm of the setting.

Accessories and props are sometimes combined to make a decoration. Candelabra can be decorated with little wreaths of miniature fruit, flowers, or fresh greens, and for weddings, garlands of delicate string smilax look pretty leading from the candelabra to the cake, which must, of course, form the centerpiece.

Place cards may be needed for a formal dinner party where more than eight guests are to be seated. These cards can be placed on the napkin (across the service plate) or in a convenient spot at the top of the setting in a decorative holder.

OPPOSITE: When a Christmas tree dominates a dining room and the table is set only for two, there is neither the space nor the necessity for a table decoration.

A centerpiece of English garden roses in an alabaster urn.

11.
How to Set the Table

A table should be set with beauty, convenience, smooth service, and comfort in mind. How casual or formal the setting looks is for the hostess to decide. Today, fortunately, we do not have the problems that faced the hostess at the end of the nineteenth century, when it was the fashion to crowd each place setting with rows of knives, forks, and spoons. Even in our grandmothers' day a complete service for twelve could include from 300 to 500 individual pieces — down to the terrapin fork — and the rules and regulations about where to place this fork or that spoon were complicated, to say the least.

Before considering the actual setting of the table, the hostess should check such details as ventilation and lighting. Both are essential and usually taken for granted as being satisfactory for everyday dining, but a more crowded room needs checking for ventilation, and the lighting should be as soft as possible, yet adequate. Ample space is important, too, for smooth service is of paramount importance. The dining-room table, whether it is oval, oblong, or round, is a very special piece of furniture, and its form and material will dictate your choice of much that goes on it. A sideboard or buffet should not be too deep, especially if the room is not large. Serving tables or a serving cart on wheels can be very convenient and make maidless serving easier.

The guiding rules for setting a table are these:

1. Handsome tables can be laid without benefit of a cloth or mats, so that the polished wood is enjoyed. However, this calls for perfect service to avoid noise, and the elimination of hot plates that will mark the surface.

2. Table linen is always correct and is varied enough to suit all tastes. Conventional tablecloths can be purchased in a wide variety of fabrics and colors. Less conventional linen can be individually designed by the clever hostess from yard goods in colors and designs that enhance both her dining room and china. Expensive tables, either old or new, and glass-topped tables, often need a "sound, or silence, cloth" to protect them and alleviate noise. You can make one of cotton felt slightly smaller than your cloth size, or purchase a cotton pad intended for this purpose.

The damask cloth is supposed to have gone out of fashion with aspidistras, but many homes still have one or two, and they remain available on the market. The quality of damask has far outlasted its fashionable value, but the frugal spirit and the ingenuity of many housewives have been responsible for its turning up in the most surprising and attractive settings, where it has been dyed to complement a color scheme.

Damask, linen, madeira, and organdy involve the fine art of laundering. This has become a very expensive item in entertaining, so it is better to use table mats in the same fine fabrics instead of a cloth. Mats also permit the enjoyment of the table itself. The market has mats in every conceivable fabric and texture to go with every type of setting. I have used plastic mats (made in Italy) that are so fine and light that a connoisseur of fine fabrics thought they were Belgian lace. Most of us would love to own Belgian lace mats, but I doubt that they would see much use because of the very special care they require. These plastic substitutes need only very casual laundering and, of course, no ironing. Many mat sets come in traditional designs with a long center "runner," but this seldom enhances the centerpiece and tends to make the table look "busy." On the other hand, decorating magazines have shown table settings using a variety of table scarves and unusual runners ranging from floral patterns in yard goods to Chinese stoles, and the effects have been most glamorous.

For comfort and elegance, the tablecloth should overhang from 10 to 12 inches. In the case of banquet tables, the overhang should be 15 inches or longer. Needless to say, all table linen should be kept spotlessly clean and well pressed.

3. For family service, every household will have established a regular pattern for seating. When guests are expected, 24 inches should be allowed for each place setting. For very formal dinners, and in Europe, where a side plate is often used, 30 inches should be allowed. A crowded table is uncomfortable and makes service difficult. A setting for the individual at the table is referred to as a "place setting." For professional service in restaurants and at banquets in Europe and America the place setting is termed the "cover."

LEFT: Silver placement is for convenience, since the first pieces to be used are on the outside of the place setting or cover. All forks are at the left of the service plate except the oyster fork, and knives and spoons are on the right.

OPPOSITE: In most European countries dessert silver is on the table at the beginning of the meal. In America dessert flatware (except for family meals, when it is placed with the rest of the utensils) is brought with the dessert service and finger bowl.

The seating may be the conventional plan with the host and hostess at either end, and guests placed along both sides of the table, directly facing each other. However, this depends on the size and shape of the table and the number of people to be seated. The service plate or regular dinner plate should be placed one inch in from the edge of the table. If the plate has a one-way pattern, it must, of course, be placed correctly. Bread-and-butter plates used for luncheon, informal dinners, and breakfast are placed at the left, just above the forks, where they should balance the placement of the glasses.

4. The simple rules for the placement of flatware are based on convenience. The first pieces to be used are on the outside. All forks are placed at the left of the plate, with the exception of the oyster fork. When this is needed it should go to the right of the soupspoon, since it is used only in the right hand. All knives and spoons are set to the right of the plate except the butter knife or spreader, which is placed on the bread-and-butter plate, parallel to the table edge, or else diagonally across one side. For family dinner, if tea or coffee is to be served with the main course, a teaspoon is included in the place setting.

Whatever the menu calls for, no more than three forks should be set at the left and three knives and the oyster fork at the right. If more pieces are required, they can be brought in as needed. This will avoid a cluttered appearance. Dessert flatware, except at family meals, when it is placed with the rest of the utensils, is brought with the dessert service and finger bowl. The finger bowl is set on the dessert plate, with or without a doily, and the dessert fork on the left and dessert spoon on the right. The diner, following the hostess, should remove the flatware to the table, and place the finger bowl above the fork

These diagrams represent the most widely accepted place-setting plans, but segments of every nation still follow their own traditional plans, according to the menus. For example, the fruit knife and fork and the dessert spoon and fork may be placed above the service plate, and a bread-and-butter plate added to a dinner table.

LEFT: Breakfast. 1: Cereal dish. 2: Plate. 3: Bread-and-butter plate. 4: Water tumbler. 5: Juice glass. 6: Cup and saucer. A: Napkin. B: Spreader (bread-and-butter knife). C: Fork. D: Knife. E: Cereal spoon (a cream-soup spoon is used). F: Coffee or tea spoon (if this spoon is used for grapefruit another spoon may be added to the saucer).

RIGHT: Luncheon. 1 and 2: Soup or seafood service on small plate. 3: Service plate. 4: Bread-and-butter plate. 5: Water glass. 6: Wine goblet. A: Napkin. B: Spreader. C: Fork. D: Salad fork. E: Knife. F: Soup spoon (a cream-soup spoon is used. G: Coffee or tea spoon. H: Fork for seafood cocktail (if soup is not served).

on the left. Spoons for coffee served with dessert come with the service at that time. Otherwise, when this service is set up in another room, to be served at the end of the meal, they are placed on the saucer.

The cutting edges of all knives should be turned toward the plate. Lay all flatware one inch in from the edge of the table in line with the service plate and napkin, making a neat, parallel row. The exception would be at a round table; there the row of utensils would start at the table edge, on the outside, but the last pieces to be used should be one inch in and next to the plate. Place them far enough apart for convenience, yet sufficiently close to avoid an untidy or careless appearance. A place setting should be orderly and symmetrical, with convenient room on either side for each person's comfort. The basic minimum place setting in flatware includes six pieces: knife, fork, teaspoon, soupspoon, salad fork, and butter knife or spreader. A further list, including serving pieces, is included in chapter 7.

Only the pieces required by the menu must be placed on the table. For a formal table, all the flatware usually comes from a matching service, but today many hostesses, when they are setting interesting tables for informal parties, enjoy mixing pieces that are harmonious in design.

5. Size and neatness of napkins are important. While a small napkin, or serviette, is adequate for a ladies' luncheon, men prefer a large napkin at dinnertime. For economy of time and effort, large heavyweight paper napkins can be substituted for breakfast and

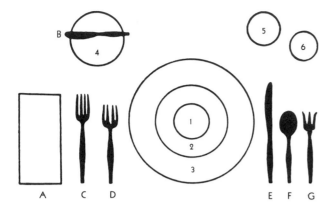

LEFT: Informal dinner. 1 and 2: Soup or sea-food cocktail service on small plate. 3: Service plate. 4: Bread-and-butter plate. 5: Water glass or goblet. 6: Wine goblet. A: Napkin. B: Spreader. C: Fork. D: Salad fork. E: Knife. F: Soup spoon. G: Seafood fork (used if soup is not served, replaced with spoon if fruit cocktail is served). (Coffee is usually served elsewhere; spoon is included with full coffee service.)

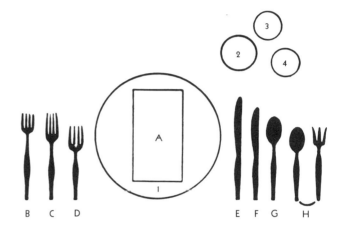

RIGHT: Formal dinner. 1: Service plate. 2: Water goblet. 3: White-wine goblet. 4: Red-wine goblet. A: Napkin (oblong shape, usually triple-fold). B: First-course fork. C: Main-course fork. D: Salad fork. E: Main-course knife. F: First-course knife. G: Soup spoon (oval bowl for formal meals and soup plates). H: Fruit-cocktail spoon or seafood fork. (Dessert silver is brought with service; coffee is usually served afterwards.)

lunch, but should never be used for a sit-down dinner when a guest is present. Napkins are most often selected to match the tablecloth or mats, but a contrasting color and texture can sometimes make a setting come to life. Fancy folds are for fancy parties and special events. Most commonly used is the simple oblong fold, with corners neatly together on the lower left and the decorated corner or monogram showing.

If a cold first course is already in place when the diners sit down, the napkin is correctly placed at the left of the forks. Otherwise, the napkin may be placed across the dinner plate, except for formal dinners and banquets, when it is always placed across the service plate. Never refold a napkin at the end of a meal. Pick it up by the center, allowing the four corners more or less to fall together, and lay it on the table to the left of the place setting so that it looks as flat and tidy as possible.

6. Although in Europe a water glass is optional, in America it is always placed on the table, slightly above the tip of the knife, and is filled with iced water before guests are seated. Other glasses are, of course, determined by the beverages to be served, and are placed to the right of the water glass. If there are two or more extra glasses, the first to be used is slightly forward, and nearest the diner. When three glasses are used, they are usually placed in a triangle. If more than three glasses are needed, they should be added at the right moment rather than overcrowding the normal place setting. At state banquets and large affairs, where more space is allowed, there is room for a fourth glass. Several pictures,

American and European, show banquets set for royalty, with as many as seven glasses at each place setting. These were needed for the many different wines served at special functions of this kind and were placed on the table to save complicated and disturbing service. On formal tables, glasses are usually of matched crystal, but many informal settings are enhanced by a water glass in a solid color.

7. Individual salts and peppers go at the top of the service plate, but generally speaking, one set between each two places is considered enough. Cigarette and match holders are a necessity if you know that your guests are likely to want to smoke during dinner. These go at the top of the place setting, too, giving sufficient reason for not using individual salt and pepper shakers.

Place cards for a large dinner party are placed flat on the napkin or in a special decorative holder, wherever convenient.

Candles add flattering light, charm, elegance, and height to the table. One candle per person is not overdoing it. Even then, balanced wall sconces or buffet candelabra are usually still needed to light a dining room properly. Whatever the height of the candlesticks or candelabra, the candle flame must, as stated earlier, be above eye level for the meal. Generally speaking, candles flank the centerpiece, to make a balanced setting. This is not a rigid rule (perhaps no rule should be considered rigid where decoration is concerned), and it will depend on the shape and size of your table, and the type of decoration you plan. For instance, a round table seating five persons might have a central candelabrum (five candles) with a garland or wreath around its base.

Candlelight is used only after dusk, and it is best to light the candles at the last minute, just before everyone is seated.

8. Whether the decorations are made after putting on the linen or after the table is set is immaterial. I prefer to do it last, so that the area to be used can be gauged more easily. Chapter 9 deals with centerpieces in detail. Fresh flowers are the first choice of most hostesses, but well-selected artificial silk, cotton, or plastic flowers, fruit, decorative vegetables, and handsome ceramic pieces are among the innumerable things that can be arranged with taste. It is important to keep centrally placed decorations low for easy cross-table conversation. When fresh material is used, the water level in the container should be such that there is no fear of spilling or leakage, yet enough to keep the flowers fresh. A happy meal should not be spoiled by a marred table top or tablecloth. The decoration is the most changeable part of a table setting and the one area where creative ability can really alter the whole effect. The photographs on pages 96 and 97, showing different tables set with the same china, demonstrate this point.

9. Our busy lives and a growing desire for simplicity and informality have been re-

OPPOSITE: Tall mixed bouquets look lovely on the sideboard or buffet table. There should be variety in form, and the colors should harmonize. A mixed "Flemish" bouquet like this finds its own shape as flowers are added. Tall spikes are set high.

A kitchen breakfast table set with gay color helps to start the day cheerfully. The table incorporates a "lazy Susan" revolving center for easy service.

sponsible for the popularity of buffet settings. These are used equally for luncheons, teas, dinners, suppers, and picnics. The guiding principle here is a well-balanced and appetizing-looking table arrangement, planned so that guests can help themselves conveniently from dishes with nearby serving pieces. Dinnerware, flatware, and napkins are usually placed in an effective pattern at a central point so that progression of service is obvious. Hot food should be very hot, cold food should be very cold, and both should be kept that way through the service. Young people do not mind what the seating arrangements are, but most men and older people appreciate separate trays or card tables set up wherever convenient so that they can sit properly when eating. Balancing a plate on one's knee and a coffee cup on the arm of a chair is not conducive to comfort and good digestion, and very often results in embarrassing spills. Card tables may be set in advance so that guests have to carry only their plates of food. This, too, allows more space on the dining table or buffet for food containers, platters, serving pieces, and decorations. China, napkins, coffee service, and dessert may be set up on the buffet with flatware for each service, leaving the table less crowded. The whole plan should be worked out for the convenience and comfort of the guests, with a desire to make them feel at ease.

In many countries, asbestos mats or pads are used under hot dishes. Many are decorated with scenes and floral designs, others are covered by table mats. Either way I feel that they spoil the look of the setting, especially when the table is cleared for dessert. Their practical use — to prevent very hot plates from marring the table — should not be necessary, for no plate should ever come to the table so hot that the place mat itself does not provide sufficient protection. Their utilitarian value in no way makes up for their lack of good design and suitability.

In England the place setting at formal dinners is wider than in America, for it includes a side plate for bread, and, as fish is a popular course, a fish knife and fork. The dessert spoon and fork which were always found above the place setting (spoon bowl to the left, fork tines to the right) are now often set with the rest of the flatware. In France and other European countries, many private homes still set the fork tines and the spoon bowls down, as on page 127, and the older families, particularly in France, still use knife rests. The custom of serving many courses, even at a family dinner when a full complement of silver was not laid out, made the rest necessary as a support for the used knife and fork during the changing of service (see pages 127 and 149). And, as it is the custom to eat fresh fruit as a course after dessert, the fruit knife and fork are included in the flatware selection.

In England, serviettes are usually laid across the service plate, owing probably to the wider place setting. However, if the first course is in place, the serviette is put on the bread plate, often with the butter knife on top. In Sweden and other northern European countries, it is often the custom to fold and pleat napkins and place them decoratively in beer

glasses, which are frequently used on luncheon and informal tables in place of water glasses.

In Italy there seems to be no particular rule about the placement of the napkin: sometimes it is on the right, sometimes on the left, and sometimes across the plate. Italians also are flexible about the placement of glassware. Sometimes it is found in a row on the right side with the center glass at the top of the knife, and, perhaps more often, across the top of the place setting in the manner of other formal European dinner tables.

As stated before, the water glass is not a "must" in Europe as it is in America, but a question of preference, decided by the hostess. In Mediterranean countries bottled water of different kinds is usually offered at mealtime, the glass being brought in at the time of service. Although candlesticks and candelabra are not used to the extent that they are in the New World, when they are used, they can be the most exquisite decorations one can imagine, as on page 181.

Open salt dishes are used more in England and on the Continent than in America, and finger bowls are in more general use, owing to the custom of eating fruit as a final course.

I have always found a greater enjoyment and awareness of the beauty of flowers on the dining table in England than on the Continent, where fruit, more often than not, becomes the centerpiece and decoration. In Italy and France fine ceramic and porcelain pieces are also very popular as centerpieces, and they are always a good decoration in the winter months, when flowers are scarce.

Detail of a fresco by Luca Signorelli from the life of St. Benedict.

12.

Table Etiquette

The importance of politeness has never been ignored. As Ralph Waldo Emerson observed, "Their first service is very low, — when they are minor morals; but, 'tis the beginning of civility, — to make us, I mean, endurable to each other. . . . Men take each other's measure, when they meet for the first time, — and every time they meet. . . . Defect in manners is usually the defect of fine perceptions."

English aristocracy had long before Emerson engaged in learning correct behavior from France, which, since the age of chivalry, had been Europe's chief instructor in courtesy. "Even the outward motions imply a certain kindliness and consideration for others," as Arthur Schlesinger has pointed out in *Learning How to Behave*. "Nor, except for the tyro, do the commandments complicate social life nearly as much as they simplify it." It is this simplification of life which is so helpful. In the words of Margery Wilson in her *Pocket Book of Etiquette*, "It is a wonderful comfort to have islands of certainty to swim to when one plunges out from self into society. The more we put recurring movements into form, the more mind we have left for spontaneous living that is refreshing and pleasant."

Thus, the subject of manners and table etiquette was given much time and thought long ago by many eminent men. In the fourteenth century, in his *Canterbury Tales,*

Chaucer reveals almost the whole character of the prioress by the mere description of her eating habits:

> At table neat and nicely bred withal,
> She let no morsel from her fair lips fall,
> Nor dipped her fingers in the sauce too deep;
> Well could she lift her portion and well keep,
> So that no fragment fell upon her breast.
> For manners meet she had a gentle zest,
> Her quaffing lips she ever wiped so clean
> That on her cup no smallest spot was seen
> Of tell-tale grease, when she had emptied it;
> She stretched her hand for food with temperance fit . . .

In Europe, in the late fifteenth century, there was a definite rule that it was wrong to grab food with two hands and that meat should be taken with three fingers and not too much put in the mouth at the same time. There was, however, a common joke in the early sixteenth century that three fingers in the salt could be taken as the sign of a villain — for salt, owing to its preciousness, was to be taken from the cellar with a knife. It was also not considered good manners to lick greasy fingers or rub them on a jacket instead of using a piece of bread or a napkin.

Americans born in the elite circle in the seventeenth century had the charming custom of wearing elaborate and highly fashionable hats to dinner, a custom dating from fourteenth-century Europe and shown in the pictures on page 15. Hats were removed only when a toast was given; to be uncovered at meals was, until the eighteenth century, not etiquette.

In the mid-eighteenth century, however, the eating habits of the lower classes in many countries, including America, were still on a rather primitive level. Farmers and their families stood around the table while they served themselves with a wooden spoon from a large wooden bowl. They took their meat in their fingers and put it on a piece of bread that was used as a trencher, then ate it sitting or standing anywhere in the room. Fingers and knives were the tools, and forks were by no means commonplace. According to Helen Sprackling's book *Customs on the Table Top*, an Englishwoman traveling in America in 1827 wrote to her sister that "Americans, male and female, were invariable and indefatigable eaters with their knives."

Still, some distinctions were made by those who cared to do things properly, as noted in *The School of Good Manners*, by Eleazar Moody: "Bite not thy bread, but break it; but not with slovenly fingers nor the same wherewith thou takest up thy meat. Dip not thy knife upright in thy hand, but sloping and lay it down at thy right hand, with the blade upon the plate."

"The Banquet," a painting by a fifteenth-century pupil of

By 1770 forks were more commonly used. No one had to worry about which fork to use, for there was only one, placed at the left of the plate with the tines turned down. The knife, with rounded spatulate blade, was on the right. The good trencherman, who had used his knife for everything and ignored his two-pronged fork for quite a while, gradually gave way before a growing social self-consciousness besieged by continual criticism.

Etiquette books came out with varied instructions. In 1802 another edition of *The School of Good Manners* instructed: "Let your fore-fingers be upon the back of your knife, and towards the tines of your fork, hanging down. When you lay your knife and fork down, let the points of each be upon the edge of your plate." Resistance to the fork was

Botticelli illustrating a tale from Boccaccio's *Decameron*.

still present, however, in the United States, and not just among the plainer classes.

Mrs. Farrar, the wife of a Harvard professor and author of *The Young Lady's Friend*, published in Boston in 1836, took up the argument saying:

> If you wish to imitate the French or English, you will put every mouthful into your mouth with your fork; but if you think as I do that Americans have as good a right to their own fashions as the inhabitants of any other country, you may choose the convenience of feeding yourself with your right hand armed with a steel blade; and provided you do it neatly and do not put in large mouthfuls, or close your lips tight over the blade, you ought not to be considered as eating ungenteelly.

"The Courtesan at Her Table," a medieval Franco-Flemish manuscript painting, shows the courtesan wearing not only a hat but mittens as well.

Thus, the argument waged between the various etiquette arbiters, with the fork's advocates claiming that safety and refinement both "recommended the primacy of the fork." The fork obviously won, but not without a battle.

Women (and men) in America were determined to handle their social responsibilities in a manner suitable to their station in life and consistent with the possibility of betterment. Catherine Sedgwick, writing on *Morals of Manners* in 1846, noted that "It is not here as in the old world, where one man is born with a silver spoon, and another with a pewter one, in his mouth. You may all handle silver spoons, if you will. That is, you may all rise to places of respectability."

This urge to be cultivated met with all sorts of annoying habits to be overcome. One that received criticism was haste in consuming food and another was lack of conversation at mealtimes. The fashionable also criticized those who emphasized their remarks by a touch of the foot. They pointed out the "uncouthness of sleeping in company," as well as the equally urgent obligation of not putting people to sleep. "Only the half-educated thought that long words and high-sounding phrases were distingué. . . ." On the other hand, the woman whose mind was "bounded on the north by her servants, on the east by her children, on the south by her ailments, and on the west by her clothes" was greatly reprehended by those around her.

Keeping up with all the so-called established injunctions involved a certain amount of strain. It meant memorizing many rules, such as: ". . . remove one's gloves before eating . . . unfold the napkin and, in the case of a woman, pin it to one's belt; . . . chew noiselessly; . . . sop up juices with pieces of bread; . . . avoid watching fellow guests dispatch their food; . . . cease conversation with the lady at your side if she should raise an unmanageable portion to her mouth."

Interest in the tea ceremony, however, brought things to a head; the foreigner who wished to participate *had* to learn the rules. One Frenchman, Monsieur de Castellus, writing about the tea party given by a Mrs. Robert Morris in Philadelphia, notes, ". . . the hostess continues to fill up the teacups unless they are reversed, and the spoon put on top." Prince de Broglie records his unhappy ignorance of that rule: "I partook of most excellent tea and I should be even now still drinking it, I believe, if the Ambassador had not charitably notified me at the twelfth cup that I must put my spoon across it."

Today we are amused by the eighteenth-century English custom that required "the women to come in to dinner with the first dish and to go out after dinner with the first glass," the first glass being a toast to exiled Prince Charlie. This custom of excusing the ladies in order to toast one another dates back to the seventeenth century. The segregated enjoyment of gay stories, pipes, and port has more or less passed from the social scene, but wine drinking and its accouterments are still very much with us, although many pieces of the early eighteenth-century equipage are no longer used. Wine glasses, for instance, used

to be cooled in a large monteith. Later, individual wine coolers or water-glasses appeared, having one or two lips to support the stem of the glass while the bowl was cooled in the ice water.

These coolers were often confused with finger bowls and tumblers. Actually finger bowls were made to match water-glasses and were referred to as "wash hand glasses" in the mid-eighteenth century. Later the name "washer" was preferred. By the end of the century they were known as finger-cups, finger-basins, and finger-glasses — and finally as finger bowls, half a century after that.

Originally, the bowls served the double purpose of cleansing the fingers and rinsing the mouth at the end of the meal. In 1788 an etiquette book gave instructions for the butler "to put on those glasses (finger bowls) half-full of clean water, when the table is cleared, but before the cloth is removed for dessert." In the early nineteenth century, diluted rose water and sometimes eau de cologne were used instead of water. When they were not placed for individual use they were passed down each side of the table so that guests could dip the corners of their napkins in them and refresh both the lips and fingertips.

In America in the early nineteenth century, folded napkins (usually a sort of "cozy" for bread), cutlery, wine glasses, and finger bowls were seen on fashionable tables. The Continental style of using the knife and fork in separate hands did not find favor in America, and the reason for this is obscure. It is interesting to note, however, that despite original resistance to the fork — it was thought a most "comical" tool when first intro-

174

duced — it eventually became the most-used tool on the American table. There were still warnings, of course, against eating with a knife, for habit dies hard, and the cult of the spoon was forever conflicting with that of the fork. In *Learning How to Behave,* in 1887, one authority on manners wrote, "The true devotee of fashion does not dare to use a spoon except to stir his tea or to eat his soup with, and meekly eats his ice-cream with a fork and pretends to like it." In 1898 common sense came to the rescue: "It is in order now to eat ice-cream and berries with a spoon, also puddings and sauces."

The end of the nineteenth century and the beginning of the twentieth were periods of great pomp and circumstance; a fashionable guest found himself faced with "a bewildering number of glass goblets, wine and champagne glasses, several forks, knives, and spoons, and a majolica plate holding oysters on the half shell." At formal functions, from five to eighteen courses were served, involving hours of eating. To cut down on this agony, a Russian custom was introduced whereby the host neither carved nor served, for his servants carried the food from the pantries according to a menu. Etiquette writers of the time pointed out, "Both host and guest are relieved from every kind of responsibility. Dish after dish comes round, as if by magic; and nothing remains but to eat and be happy." This method also opened the door to professional caterers, and the socially overworked or inexperienced hostess could order a party as she did a bonnet.

Fine points of dining were still discussed, and advice on delicate matters, such as removal of hairs or insects from one's dish, continued to be published. Etiquette books sold in the millions, including those by Lilian Eichlet and Emily Post. Mrs. Post warned Americans, "What is regarded as highly ill-bred now may be acceptable before you have finished reading this book."

Friendly, informal parties became the rule and not the exception. Cocktails, which had been served occasionally before dinner earlier in the century, now became a matter of course, with relishes and other attractive tidbits accompanying them.

Enormous dinner parties requiring a bevy of servants and a fortune in tableware were similarly giving way to smaller, simpler affairs. The successful hostess became "not she who can display the richest silver, but she who can make her guests feel comfortable and happy." Etiquette is, after all, little more than a sincere consideration for others. For this reason, lateness is pardonable only when it is unavoidable, and a phone call to your host or hostess is obligatory. A hostess may be expected to wait only twenty minutes before going ahead with dinner.

Regarding seating at the table, the woman guest of honor sits at the host's right and is served first. The next woman guest of importance sits at the host's left. Similarly, the men of honor or those to be given special preference sit on the right and left of the hostess.

An eighteenth-century French dining room with side "service" tables.

13.
Service –
with and without Help

Designers and manufacturers have produced all kinds of machinery and gadgets to make cooking and serving meals increasingly easy, but the human element is, and always will be, all-important to the success of a party. The extent to which help is available, and can be accommodated and afforded, separates us, roughly speaking, into three groups, each posed with a slightly different problem of entertaining at home.

The limited number of people who, in these days, can command a trained staff, represents one group. The second can be said to be those who have household help or use a catering service, and the last and largest group are the hosts who have no help at all except the family and understanding guests. In each category, planning is equally essential. Successful entertaining does not just happen, although it is true that the impromptu, informal party, given without any preliminary fuss and bother, does often turn out to be the most enjoyable of all.

A well-balanced meal, planned so that it keeps as hot (or as cold) as it was meant to be, that is served correctly and with ease to appreciative company in an attractive setting, is the obvious aim of every hostess. The experienced housewife already knows the answers and how far she is prepared to go to achieve her ideals, but to those just setting up housekeeping, the following check list suggests what can be expected from the kind of space and help you have or can hire for a sit-down dinner party.

TRAINED HELP IN LARGE HOUSEHOLDS

1. The size of the guest list is usually established by the size of the staff — six guests to each person serving.

2. The time for dinner, and the time for guests to arrive for cocktails, is settled. Invitations are written or telephoned, with a reminder sent later in the mail to busy people and new friends who need to have your address, phone number, and directions.

3. The menu is discussed and written out for the cook or chef. Formal dinners today usually do not exceed four courses, preceded by cocktails with canapés or hors d'oeuvres.

4. Cocktails may be made to order in the pantry (or kitchen) and served on a tray. It should be possible to serve hot hors d'oeuvres if you have a trained staff; otherwise, canapés and dip dishes are quite sufficient.

5. Before guests enter the dining room, water glasses should be filled, butter, if needed, placed on the butter plates, and candles lighted.

6. The servant should catch the eye of the hostess and announce when dinner is served. For a small group, the hostess seats the guests; otherwise, seating is indicated by place cards. The female guest of honor sits on the host's right, other honored guests on his left and on either side of the hostess, women alternating with men.

7. After the guests are seated, the first course is brought in on an accompanying plate and placed on the service plate before them. The service plate is never, at any time thereafter, left empty; as one course is removed, another takes its place.

8. All serving of food is done on the guest's left side, and water and wine on the right. Service begins with the guest on the host's right and proceeds around the table counterclockwise. If two people are serving, they should begin at the right and left of the host and proceed down the table, then serving the host and hostess, who immediately picks up the outside piece of flatware (on right of setting) as a signal for the guests to begin eating.

9. The first course is removed with the left hand, and the warm fish course plate is substituted with the right hand. The fish course is served with white wine.

10. The second course is removed with the service plate while a warm plate is substituted with the right hand. The hot entrée is served from garnished platters — often with accompanying potatoes. Other vegetables follow in partitioned dishes. The sauces and red wine are served. At a formal dinner nothing is offered a second time except water and wine replenishments. Individual servings of salad should be placed to the left of the guests if the menu requires them.

11. Remove the main course. Remove salt, pepper, unused flatware, and empty wine glasses to a small tray (leaving the water glass and the glass for dessert wine). Fill the water glasses (never touch the glass and use a napkin in case of drips).

12. Bring in the dessert plate, doily, and finger bowl (and the flatware also if it is not already on the table). The guest puts the doily and finger bowl to the left of the setting and puts his flatware in place on the table. Dessert accompanied by sweet wine or champagne is served.

13. The hostess makes the first move to leave by putting her unfolded napkin at the left of her setting.

14. A servant brings the coffee equipment into the living room for the hostess to pour. The servant passes the coffee to the guests. Liqueurs and glasses are brought in on a tray and served as requested.

During dinner, a servant removes any debris left after the cocktail party and tidies the living room. If the dinner party is larger than twelve and a full complement of staff is not available, the removal of each course begins when the majority has finished. But no guest should be made to feel hurried.

RESIDENT MAID OR HIRED HELP

1. Usually six to eight guests are invited.

2. The time for cocktails and dinner is settled. Invitations are written or telephoned.

3. The menu is written out for the maid to check the procedure. A resident maid will know where things are and your way of doing things. Hired help will need everything put out in readiness and a more careful check of procedure. Remember to allow plenty of room around the table for service. Usually a three-course dinner is offered. Canapés and dips that do not need constant attention are suggested.

4. Cocktails may be mixed and served at a bar accommodation in the living room or in any other suitable place. The maid serves the canapés.

5. Before the guests enter the dining room, the water glasses should be filled, butter put on the butter plates, and candles lighted. Sherry should be poured if it is to be served with the first course.

6. The maid announces to the hostess that dinner is served at a prearranged time or twenty minutes after the last guest has arrived. The hostess seats guests in the customary manner of alternation, unless one sex outnumbers the other, and then the hostess uses her discretion.

7. To simplify service, the first course may be already on the table, whether it is a cold fruit cup or a hot soup in covered dishes.

8. All serving of the food is done on the left side of the guest. Water and wine are served on the right.

OPPOSITE: Special dinner parties inspire special decorations. This floral idea is popular in many countries. The size of the table decoration is often gauged by the space available after the table is fully set, but here it is immaterial as the flowers are high above the cloth and so arranged as not to interfere with the conversation of the guests. The container for the flowers is a circular one made especially to fit around the center of the candelabrum.

9. Service begins with the guest on the host's right, and then it should proceed around the table counterclockwise. When the hostess is served, she picks up the appropriate flatware as a signal for her guests to begin eating.

10. The carving may be done at the table if there is room and the host is so inclined, or done by him in the kitchen at a convenient moment. While this is taking place, the first-course dishes with the service plate are removed and a warm dinner plate substituted, so that guests may then help themselves from the platters and dishes as they are taken around by the maid. On the other hand, the hostess may do all the serving, using a service cart or side table for the vegetables and sauces, with the maid taking the main course to each person. Wine may be served by a servant or the host. Salad may be placed on the table at the left of each setting or may be mixed at the table by the hostess and then passed by the guests.

11. Remove the main course. Remove salt, pepper, unused flatware, and empty wine glasses to a small tray. Fill the water glasses, empty or replace the ashtrays, and crumb the table.

12. A dessert plate should be brought to each guest and the dessert served by the maid.

13. The hostess makes the first move to leave by putting her unfolded napkin on the left of her setting.

14. A servant brings the coffee tray with service into the living room for the hostess to pour. The maid may take coffee to the guests or allow them to get it themselves. Liqueurs and glasses may be in readiness on a table for the host to serve, as well as any liquids other than coffee.

During dinner, a maid or member of the family removes any remains of the cocktail service, and tidies the living room.

DINNER SERVICE WITH NO OUTSIDE HELP
Plan One
1. The number to be entertained depends upon the number in the family who can help. A wise mother has a well-trained family staff.

2. Two days prior to the dinner party, make a detailed timetable of things to be done.

3. The menu should be interesting, in season, well balanced, and made up of those dishes you do best and which require as little complication in the service as possible. Avoid dishes that need constant attention, such as hot hors d'oeuvres, hot soup, steak, baked Alaska, or a soufflé.

OPPOSITE: If collapsible tray tables are used, a meal can be served anywhere — in the living room, as shown in the top illustration, by the fireside, or on the porch. A second illustration demonstrates that a menu that can be served at the table or from a nearby buffet saves trips to the kitchen and does not disturb the continuity of conversation and service.

4. Cocktails and other drinks may be served by the host from a convenient place: a portable bar, a bar cart, or a small table set up with all the equipment necessary. Dip dishes, stuffed celery, carrot strips, etc., are easy to prepare and to serve.

5. As informal dinner without maid service is more casual, the first course may be cold and in place on the service plates before the guests enter the dining room. This allows more leisure time for cocktails. At the last minute, fill the water glasses, put butter on the butter plates, if necessary, and light the candles.

6. A roast or casserole is easy to serve and to keep hot. The host with carving skill and room at the table will need carving tools and their supports, or other serving pieces, and warm dinner plates. The service plates will have been removed with the first course.

The serving of vegetables is a problem. They may be served by the host from a small side table at his left (rather than have them crowd the dining table) or a member of the family can do this, taking the filled plate to each guest. Another plan is to have the host carve the roast beforehand in the kitchen. The hostess then does all the serving from her end of the table while the host pours the wine. Another member of the family can then clear the first course, refill the water glasses, and place the salad at the left of each setting.

If there is no one to do this, a tea wagon or two-tiered serving cart eliminates any unnecessary jumping up from the table. The plates from the first course (service plate, plate and dish of the first course) are passed down the table and put on the lower shelf of the wagon. The top level is for the vegetable dishes and serving flatware. A buffet or side table is a great convenience for serving the salad, the dessert course, and coffee. A small tray placed inside the kitchen door or near at hand, is used after the main course to remove salt, pepper grinder, and unused flatware. It may hold a plate and napkin for crumbing the table if necessary. The service cart is then wheeled into the kitchen. (This may be necessary after the first course if more than six are at dinner and the wagon is small.)

7. Dessert plates are brought in and the dessert served by the hostess either from her place at table or from the buffet.

8. The coffee service is taken into the living room and hot coffee is brought when the hostess is ready to serve it and her guests are ready to enjoy it leisurely.

Plan Two

If your dinner party is for more than six and there is no family to help, set the table in the normal fashion with the cold first course or hot soup in covered dishes at each place, and have all the food for the main course arranged on a buffet table for the guests to help themselves. Hot food will need to be brought to the buffet after the first course is removed, unless it is in chafing dishes or in covered dishes on a hotplate. A side table will hold the dessert and coffee services, or they will have to be brought in to the buffet when it is cleared of the main course.

Plan Three

If your guest list is large and everyone cannot be seated conveniently around the table, the popular plan is to use your dining table to set up the buffet with duplicate service on either side, and to have bridge tables and individual tray tables set up with cloths, napkins, and flatware in the living room or another attractive setting. The first course may then consist of canapés and dip dishes to be served with the cocktails. If a salad is served with the hot course, you will need to have an extra pile of plates next to the salad bowl. Dessert may be prepared and set on the buffet or side table, or placed on the dining table when the main course has been removed. A tray of cheeses is a simple substitute for a sweet dessert. Coffee is served conveniently when everything used has been removed to the kitchen. For large informal buffets when tables cannot be used, it is best to serve meals that need only a fork, such as a casserole. After the meal the hostess takes the plates, two at a time, to the kitchen, or arranges for the guests to put them on a side table near the buffet setting.

A dinner for twenty-four people can run smoothly with two buffet settings. The table is set for twelve on either side, and the main course is in the two covered English Regency silver dishes. Dessert service and wine glasses are set out on the second buffet or sideboard.

For the family meal with close friends and no help with service or carving, the customary pattern generally adopted in the majority of households is that all carving and serving is done in the kitchen. Modern kitchens are usually designed to be attractive places to work and spacious enough for the maidless home to manage this arrangement graciously.

For those who find dinner parties of any kind too much to cope with alone, entertaining is sensibly reduced to what they can do well. For instance, if you make an exciting dessert, have friends in for just dessert and coffee. Over the Christmas holidays, the wassail bowl, eggnog with fruitcake, or Christmas cookies provide a simple plan to get friends together. Porch, patio, or garden picnics may be planned with food that does not have service problems.

In city or suburban communities, a progressive party is enjoyable. For this plan, four hostesses might get together and plan a party in four stages. The first hostess serves canapés and cocktails. The second serves the first course, which might be hot or cold soup or a special fish concoction that will keep while the cocktail party progresses and until the guests reach her house. The third hostess is responsible for the main course. The fourth home provides the dessert, coffee, and liqueurs. Many groups, having found this plan successful, make it a regular monthly custom, with the hostesses serving the various courses in turn. In this manner one has a continuing arrangement for seeing friends and keeping up with local events of interest, the work involved is kept at a minimum for each hostess, and the moving from house to house provides an amusing change of pace, especially during the summertime.

LEFT: A serving cart is very useful for families who entertain without help. Glasses, drinks, and canapés can be set out in the kitchen before the guests arrive and then transferred to the most convenient place for serving.

OPPOSITE: A dining table set for a buffet meal in Switzerland. The collection of pewter *channes* dates from 1708. The *channes* were mostly used for wine, and each canton has its own particular shape.

An eighteenth-century engraving of a French family enjoying *vin du pays*.

14.
Wine and
Its Service

Nothing goes so well with good food or goes so well into the making of good food as wine: like a flower and a leaf, food and wine complement each other perfectly. In Europe many people drink wine with every meal; in England, and especially in America, wine is usually reserved for dinner and parties. But there are connoisseurs everywhere whose understanding and devotion to its perfection might be termed almost a cult.

Red wines are made from red grapes, or black grapes, as they are sometimes described. During fermentation, the skins are left on the fruit, and as the wine ferments in the vats, the alcohol formed dissolves the pigment in the skins, giving the wine its color.

White wines are made from either red grapes or white (actually they are green), and the skins are removed before fermentation.

Champagnes come from the Pinot Noir, a black grape. The juice is pressed from the grape and fermented without the skins and pulp.

Rosé wines are made by fermenting the juice with the skins until the wine achieves the approved degree of pinkness. Then the skins are removed.

All fine vintage wines, those we buy in the market, will have been bottled at the estate of origin by the grower himself. This is a guarantee of authenticity and, it follows, of quality. A wine grower's reputation rests entirely on his wines. Consequently, if he produces a

OPPOSITE: Eighteenth-century conviviality. A detail of the "Oyster Meal" by Jean-François de Troy.

vintage that fails to meet his standard, he will not bottle it under his own label but will sell it to a shipper for blending with other wines. Therefore, as a general rule, the more specifically the label pinpoints the place of origin, the finer the wine will be.

All wines are vintage wines unless they are blended — their vintage is the year they were produced. Vintage is important only in quality wines, not in those for everyday consumption or cooking. But it is fairly rare now for wine growers to have a really poor year, owing to modern techniques of vinification, so "vintage" used in this sense is becoming less important except for the most ardent connoisseurs. Although "vintage wine" has come to be applied only to a superb wine, the age on the label of the bottle is important in telling us when the wine is ready for drinking. As a rule, dry white wines, rosés, and some red wines, such as Beaujolais, taste best when they are young, while the greater red wines require more aging to reach perfection.

So much ritual has come to surround the service and tasting of wine that many potential drinkers are intimidated. However, rules based on common sense should be followed. If several wines are to be served at a meal (which is not very common now), they should follow this order: an ordinary wine before a better one; a light delicate wine before a heavy, full-bodied one; a dry wine before a sweet wine; a recent vintage before an old one. There is a saying that "the wine last served should never bring regrets for the previous one."

As the temperature of wine varies, so do the qualities that predominate. The characteristics of a red wine can be better appreciated when it is served at what is commonly called room temperature. However, this phrase was established centuries ago, when huge rooms were heated only by a log fire, and certainly "room temperature" was never intended

As soon as the bottling of champagne is completed, the wine is taken down to cold cellars, where the temperature is about fifty degrees F. FAR RIGHT: Wicker tubs filled with grapes are examined by "pickers" and green, overripe, or spoiled grapes are thrown out. The best grapes are taken to the wine press in spring-upholstered carts, for the grapes should not be bruised or even shaken.

190

to mean the temperature of a present-day centrally heated dwelling. It is easy to remember that red wines, which are rich and warm in color, should taste that way. On the other hand, the temperature of white and rosé wines should agree with their delicate, cool appearance.

The approved temperature for red wines is about 60° to 65° F. White and rosé wines are served slightly chilled (around 50° F.); and an hour on the shelf of the refrigerator should be enough for most types. The sweeter the wine the more it should be chilled. Over-chilling, however, will hide the desirable features of a good wine, and ice should never be added. Champagne and other sparkling wines take longer to chill and may be left in the refrigerator on a lower shelf for two or more hours. The traditional method is to use an icebucket for slower cooling, but here the disadvantage is that the wine in the neck of the bottle often is not chilled enough unless the ice is stacked high.

Sherry is usually served at normal room temperature, although some people like it chilled, especially when it is served at cocktail hour. One wine with dinner is sufficient under most circumstances, and certainly one good wine is better than two mediocre ones. Wine is usually poured after the soup is served, or, if the first course is cold, just before the meat course is carved or passed. For special dinners when you wish to serve more than one wine, sherry is often chosen to accompany the soup course and may be poured before the guests are seated. The glass is removed when the red or white wine is served before the next course.

It is the host, rather than the hostess, who serves the wine and sees to it that glasses are replenished during the meal.

Consideration and good manners have been responsible for the pleasant custom of

first pouring a little wine into the host's glass. If there are any little pieces of cork in the wine, it is hoped that they will come into his glass rather than into those of the guests. The host's approval of the wine is the signal for it to be served — to his right — around the table, and his glass is filled last.

Wine should be poured gently, the glass only half filled so that the aroma and bouquet may be concentrated in the empty space at the top.

Only great and old wines need special handling. If the bottle contains sediment (a mark of old age and often of greatness) it should be left standing upright for a day or two after transportation until the sediment has collected at the bottom. A bottle of less distinguished wine bought on the way home or brought out from the "home cellar" can be treated more casually.

Red wine is improved if the bottle is uncorked about one hour before the meal. Thus it will absorb oxygen and start "breathing," which gives it depth and smoothness and awakens the bouquet.

On the other hand, white and rosé wines have a very delicate fragrance, the freshness of which is lost if it is exposed to air for too long a time. The bottles should therefore be opened just before serving.

ABOVE: Handsome decanters add a note of distinction to a table or buffet, but no red wine less than ten years old needs to be decanted, and a white wine rarely does. This modern Italian hand-wrought iron wine tipper holds the bottle for serving at table. RIGHT: An eighteenth-century pewter *channe*.

A French wine-tasting picnic, set in a garden on the banks of the Loire.

Champagne and sparkling wines are opened right at the table to prevent the precious bubbles from escaping too soon. After the cork is removed, the mouth of the bottle should be wiped clean with a small towel or napkin. Wine left over in a bottle after a meal may be recorked, and the wine will keep for a day or two in the refrigerator. A white or rosé wine will keep much longer than a red wine.

A good-looking, well-proportioned decanter adds a note of distinction to any table. However, there is no need to decant a red wine less than ten years old, and rarely a white wine. The object of decanting is to avoid the dregs and sediment in the bottom of the bottle, and you can do this by pouring carefully — and by leaving the last half-inch as an offering to the gods.

OPPOSITE: A Continental setting with glasses on a separate mat. The first glass (at the top of the large spoon) is for bottled water and is smaller than American water glasses, which are designed to hold ice cubes. The wine glass is set back, behind the water glass.

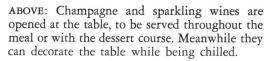

ABOVE: Champagne and sparkling wines are opened at the table, to be served throughout the meal or with the dessert course. Meanwhile they can decorate the table while being chilled.

RIGHT: Champagne and balloons decorate a New Year's Eve table.

Old wines need special handling while being transferred from the bottle to a carafe or decanter. Do it two hours before serving. First place the bottle as gently as possible in a cradle, draw the cork, and pour the wine slowly into the decanter against a light until the first sign of sediment appears. Then let it stand upright for the two hours before serving.

A wine basket is useful to carry the wine without shaking the bottle unnecessarily, but at the table the basket or cradle is purely decorative.

Wine connoisseurs have a special glass for each wine, but this is not a necessity unless your interest warrants it. Experts agree that one type of wine glass is more or less perfect for all wines, including champagne. This is a long-stemmed, tulip-shaped glass with the bowl the size of an orange. It is obvious that a real wine lover will want his glass to be crystal, clear and thin, so that he may enjoy the full, rich, glowing color of the wine; he will want the bowl large so that a half-filled glass is generous enough to be enjoyed through a course. The stem not only adds to the elegance of the glass but prevents the bowl from being warmed by the hand, and the wine therefore remains at the proper temperature. Since wine should be sipped, the glass is lifted often from the table.

Glasses are usually grouped at the top of the knives at every place setting, with the wine glasses to the right of the water glass (see Chapters 8 and 11). In France, however, they are placed at the top of the setting. For formal settings the glasses usually match; for informal and family dinners they are often mixed. The water glass may be a solid color and the wine glasses may be clear or lightly tinted. Green glass used to be a tradition for Hock Heimer and other Rhine wines, especially in Germany. Some hostesses use colored glasses just for the decorative effect. The saucer-shaped champagne glass is well known as the traditional form, but the true champagne glass is a tulip shape, tall and elongated, just wide enough for the froth and bubbles to form and frolic. The saucer-shaped champagne glass is now often used for serving sherbet and champagne cocktails.

The affinity that particular wines have with certain foods has established, for some people, the plan of serving red wines with red meat, white wines with white meat, and champagne and rosé wines with all kinds of food. However, all authorities agree that this is not inflexible and that each person should drink what he prefers with each food, for part of the pleasure is discovering and developing one's own taste preferences.

The following summary may be of help:

Dry white wine, champagne or other sparkling wine: fish, oysters, shellfish, lobsters.

A light white wine or a rosé wine: white entrée dishes.

A generous red wine, not too full bodied: white meat, roasts, and poultry.

A strong full aromatic red wine: red meat, game, and cheese.

Champagne and other sparkling wines, sweet wines: dessert.

Sweet white wine, champagne: fruit.

A thoughtful hostess who encourages informal visiting will want to keep both dry

The shape of a wine bottle indicates its contents. The silhouettes below show some classic French shapes. *Left to Right:* Bordeaux, Champagne, Burgundy and Côtes du Rhone, table wine, Alsace, Provence, Arbois. Wine connoisseurs use a special glass for each wine, but experts agree that a long-stemmed, tulip-shaped glass is perfect for all wines. RIGHT: A glass for wine from the Rhine area. CENTER RIGHT: Champagne glasses: saucer-shaped, flute-shaped, and a round bowl. FAR RIGHT: Wine glasses for red wine, white wine, and sherry.

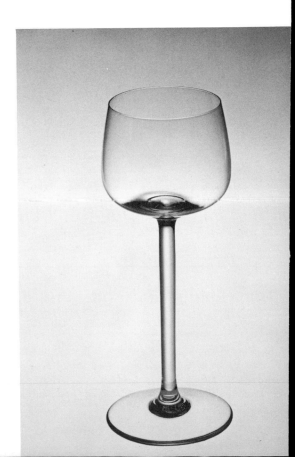

and sweet sherry, for she can serve this wine at almost any hour of the day. An attractive decanter with 6-ounce sherry glasses set on a tray on the sideboard or buffet is ready for immediate enjoyment. You may serve it before lunch, instead of afternoon tea, in place of a cocktail (either at room temperature or chilled for 30 minutes) or with soup as part of your dinner plan.

The correct storage of wine is important, but need not be an elaborate function; you have to have a cool place but not necessarily a cellar.

It is good to remember that wine is a living thing: unlike distilled liquors it is alive in the bottle. It changes as it ages and these changes need to come about under certain conditions. For instance, it is important that table wines "rest" on their sides at a slight angle so that the liquid keeps the cork moist. If you allow the bottles to stand upright, the cork will dry out and let in air that will oxidize the wine until eventually it becomes vinegar.

Your "cellar," real or improvised, should always be well ventilated, free from drafts, smells, or fumes; it should be dark, dry, potected from vibration, and away from hot-water pipes and furnaces. It might be a cool cupboard under the staircase, or part of a small box room that is cool. Wine should never be exposed to extremes in temperature; between 50° and 60° F. is preferable.

Ready-made wine racks are very helpful, for it is important to avoid all unnecessary handling or shaking of the wine.

Once started, the building up of a basic wine "cellar" can become a fascinating hobby. Be *en rapport* with your local wine merchant so that when a first-rate wine appears on the market he will notify you. You can buy it by the case at a great saving; this is a wise investment too, since such wines considerably increase in value as they age and reach maturity.

Still life. An early seventeenth-century German painting by Georg Flegel.

OPPOSITE: Chinese Export porcelain and old and new copper make an interesting background for informal meals in a large kitchen.

15.
The Changeable Hours of Mealtime

The accepted formal hours for eating have varied from century to century and from country to country, and indeed they have varied, and still vary to some degree, in each individual household. Primitive man had to eat when the hunting or fishing was good and go hungry at other times. Since then, social and economic developments have continually changed the kind of meals and mealtimes.

By the sixteenth century the French and Italians had developed elaborate, highly seasoned dishes. English fare, by comparison, was simple, although just as hearty. The Elizabethan table was a gargantuan display of meat, bird, fowl, and vegetables, and special dishes like salmagundi and peacock *pâté*.

In those days dinner was served to the upper classes at about 11 o'clock in the morning and was the day's main meal. Supper, usually the only other meal, might appear at about 5 P.M. It was considered smart to dine early, for the working classes and some merchants ate later in the day. There are also references to people breaking their fast earlier in the morning before going on a long journey or if they were ill, and to certain ladies in London who "break their fast in their beds." On occasions there were also snacks in between of bread, butter, milk, and cheese with ale or beer, that extended to "rear suppers . . . when it was time to go to rest."

Travelers ate at the inns — "ordinaries" — which supplied an assortment of snacks for those who did not bring their own food along. There were no restaurants, even in London, but one could buy pies and prepared dishes from the cooked-meat shop. From the sixteenth to the nineteenth century, courses were not served separately; several dishes would be set on the table together as part of one "remove." A dinner might involve three removes, and a banquet many more. Silver, pewter, and wooden platters were used, and the same one kept throughout the meal. Some wooden platters, flat ones, were turned over for another "remove." Poorer people used a thick slice of bread to set their food on — this absorbed the juices and was eaten at the end of the meal.

There were many changes in English and American eating habits before the present pattern began to evolve at the turn of this century. Dinner, the chief meal of the day, is ordinarily thought of as the evening meal. This was not always so. In some European countries the main meal is still taken at mid-day, while in others — particularly Spain — it is eaten after 10 P.M.

In the seventeenth century, the day began with a good, healthy breakfast. This was followed by a heavy noonday meal served at about 1 or 2 o'clock, and a comparatively light supper. In America the custom of eating supper (usually three or four hours after tea) was in keeping with the English practice of earlier decades. Among the fare served to the settlers at suppertime we read of such tidbits, mentioned by Jean McClure in her booklet, *Early American Table Settings,* as "hogs ears forced, pickled Pig's feet and ears, ox-Palates."

In farmhouses on both sides of the Atlantic, tables were "set out" with all the food at once, but in the village the squire's wife "set out two courses" in the English fashion. In city homes the two courses were extremely elaborate and offered great variety.

This habit of covering the table with platters of food was not so that each person would sample everything, but so that each would find something to his taste. Since it was considered "ungenteel" at that time for the ladies to drink more than one glass of wine,

OPPOSITE: A table set by a swimming pool is covered with a Tahitian cloth printed with hibiscus and plumeria flowers. The decorations used are shell leis and a giant clam shell filled with flaming red canna, and salvia flowers.

they retired to the drawing room or parlor after the dessert course. Later the gentlemen joined them for tea or coffee.

In 1789, when George Washington was in residence in New York, he would eat a hearty breakfast around 7:30 to 8 o'clock and nothing after that, until a substantial dinner at 3 P.M. In America, lunch did not exist in those days. Supper was eaten at 8 P.M. Clerks and other working people had their breakfast at 7 A.M., dinner at noon, and supper between 6 and 7 P.M. Outside the cities, dinner seems to have been eaten at "two o'clock P.M." In 1836 Mrs. Farrar of Massachusetts noted in her book *The Young Lady's Friend*, "A dinner, well performed by all the actors in it, is very fatiguing and, as it generally occupies three hours or more, most persons are glad to go away when it is fairly done." If tea was taken it was served in the English fashion around 6 or 7 o'clock.

Practice remained generally the same until about 1840. At this time a French innovation, *"déjeuner à la fourchette,"* was introduced as a European refinement. Philip Hone, a one-time mayor of New York, referred to a nineteenth-century custom in an article in the New York *Herald Tribune:* " . . . the company assembles at about one o'clock and partakes of coffee and chocolate, light dishes of meat, ice-cream and confectionery, with

OPPOSITE: It may be less time-consuming for a busy hostess to take breakfast to guests in their rooms than to serve breakfast at table. RIGHT: This living room, part of an old ox barn, makes a delightful setting for a tray meal.

lemonade and French and German wines." This appears to be the first record of lunch as we know it. At that time it was called a "breakfast" or a "breakfast-dinner." In England, Jane Austen had earlier written of this meal as "noonshine," and Dr. Johnson defined "nunchin" as "a piece of victuals eaten between meals." "Nuncheon" and "nunch" were soon replaced by the terms "luncheon" and "lunch." The introduction of lunch was soon to make a distinct change in meals and their hours. The dinner hour slipped from 3 P.M. to 4 P.M. and then 5 o'clock, and in 1859, when the Fifth Avenue Hotel opened on the corner of Twenty-third Street and Fifth Avenue in New York City, dinner was served at 6 P.M. and lunch at 1 P.M. In 1865 fashionable circles extended the dinner hour to 7 P.M. and in 1890 to 8 o'clock, as in England.

This was the beginning of an era of opulent dining in Europe and America when tables and dining rooms were decorated in the "grand manner" with shining damask, plush chairs, and garlands of smilax and asparagus fern everywhere. Pictures of enor-

LEFT: A Sunday-morning late breakfast or "brunch" set on a bedroom balcony overlooking an English garden.

BELOW LEFT: The scent from garden roses adds to the charm of a meal.

BELOW: Eating outdoors when the setting and the weather are perfect makes food taste like ambrosia. Luncheon by a New England stream on a bright autumn day.

mous crystal chandeliers glittering above wide banquet tables, mounds of potted plants, and serried masses of drinking glasses throw a revealing light on that period of history. Industrial development, causing the gradual dissipation of the servant class, and other pressures helped bring about the changes that eventually led to lighter meals and our present less formal eating habits.

This pattern, generally speaking, is still three meals a day (as well as tea in England), although the type of meal and its hour of service have changed. At weekends a new mealtime has been established in some households — the combination of breakfast with lunch. "Brunch" was first popularized in New Orleans, and is usually eaten in a leisurely fashion at about 11 A.M.

The first meal, breakfast, is usually less substantial than it used to be, even in England, and some people have adopted the Continental breakfast, with no cooking, but with the addition of fruit juice. Lunch, once a novelty, now is used by women for all kinds of social meetings — fashion shows, bridge parties, and business sessions. It is seldom a family meal, except on weekends and during the summer holidays. Businessmen's luncheons range from 12:30 to 3:30 P.M. but are famed for accomplishing twice as much as those same hours spent in an office.

Office workers choose their lunchtime between noon and 2 P.M.; dinnertime usually starts between 6 and 7 P.M. in America and between 7 P.M. and 8 P.M. in England. Morning and afternoon coffee or tea breaks relieve the working hours. Leisure classes in most countries still keep 8 o'clock in the evening as the ideal time for dining, especially when entertaining. Dinner is not only the most important meal of the day, but of all forms of hospitality it is the most rewarding for both the hostess and her guests.

The gathering together of family and friends, out-of-town relatives, neighbors, and business associates and the welcoming of strangers are an essential part of civilized life. Whether it is for few or for many, simple or elaborate, the purpose is always the same: to create a mood and atmosphere of warmth and good fellowship for the leisurely enjoyment of good food.

LEFT: A theater supper is often preferred to a large dinner if there is no time for a leisurely meal.

OPPOSITE: A dinner table set with a Belgian lace tablecloth, Lenox china, and garlands of flowers suspended from candelabra.

An eighteenth-century banqueting scene by William Hogarth.

16.
Casual Entertaining

BUFFETS

Benjamin Franklin, Ambassador to France between 1776 and 1785, once celebrated the Fourth of July in Paris in great style. Lacking the space, equipment and wherewithal to compete with the lavish Parisians, he had the food laid out on a long table and invited more people than could possibly be seated. The guests ate standing up, and overflowed from the house into the garden. The Ambassador called his entertainment a buffet supper, and soon the vogue for buffets spread to other countries, including his native America.

In France at this period restaurants as we now know them did not exist. However, some thirty years after Benjamin Franklin's successful party, innkeepers had begun to find it profitable to set up one-course meals on boards at one side of a dining room, where visitors could help themselves. Later, with the emergence of the great restaurants in Paris, elaborate tables and cabinets were designed to display the chef's most elegant dishes. The French called the furniture and the meal a "buffet," whether the diner served himself or was served by a waiter. Few housewives today have not availed themselves of this very practical and flexible form of entertaining.

Buffets are readily adaptable to a variety of other meals besides dinner. Breakfasts, lunches, teas, suppers, and picnics by the pool can all be planned as buffets. Of necessity, menus must be well balanced and confined to dishes that can be prepared well ahead of time and kept at the right temperature throughout the service. Casseroles, tureens, chafing dishes, and electric hotplates are useful in keeping work to a minimum during the various stages of a serve-yourself meal.

For a small party, a table can be set up against a wall, with tray tables in the living room. For a larger affair the table is usually more conveniently placed in the center of the room, with a double service arranged on each side so that two guests or more can help themselves at the same time. To supplement the tray tables, bridge tables may be set up with cloth, napkins, and flatware on a porch, or wherever extra and convenient space is available.

Dessert, coffee, and liqueurs are usually arranged on a side buffet table or a table set up especially for this purpose, or else they are brought in later to set out on the regular dining table after the main course has been cleared away.

One of the attractive features of a buffet-table arrangement lies in the symmetrical pattern created in the placement of the dishes, flatware, serving pieces, and napkins, with full consideration given to the appropriate order in which the food will be taken. The serving dishes and platters should be harmonious in color and design. Similarly, the overall color effect of flowers, cloth, and napkins should be in keeping with the decor of the room. Flower arrangements and grouped candlesticks or candelabra can be as high as good proportion will allow. Good lighting is as essential at a buffet as at any other meal as guests must be able to see what the food is and how to serve themselves. If the table lighting is insufficient on its own, light a pair of wall sconces or extra candelabra on the buffet table, or make other appropriate arrangements. Although light must be adequate, it should be kept soft, to add to the glamour of the setting.

Linen, china, glass, and flatware can be as formal or informal as the occasion may suggest. Flowers are always a lovely addition to any party table but fruit is a good substitute. For outdoor buffets, fruit and certain vegetables artistically arranged in a wicker basket or tray make a practical, heavy centerpiece that a capricious breeze is unlikely to upset.

At large parties, the self-service plan with informal seating arrangements sometimes results in overcrowding around the buffet. To ease this problem, you might consider varying the time on your invitations so that not everyone arrives at once. You can also provide bridge tables so that the men may seat their companions and proceed to fetch dinner. It is also a good plan to arrange for members of the family or hired help to offer second helpings, to take away the plates when the meal is finished, and to serve the dessert and coffee. In this way, guests already seated do not have to leave their table and interrupt their conversation.

If wine is to be served it is a good idea to place a bottle on each table for four and let one of the men serve it. The host can pour for those sitting at separate tray tables. Young married and others entertaining in relatively small apartments may decide on a "fork supper." Here the buffet meal is set up on a large serving cart (or else on a convenient table) and is eaten standing up. Naturally, this calls for a main course where only a fork is needed, and a spoon for fruit salad or ice cream. Cocktails or predinner drinks should be adequate, since pouring wine for guests who may be seated on the floor or standing can be disastrous. Where space is limited, individual flatware services can be wrapped in a napkin, placed in an oblong basket. If only spoons and forks are used, the tines and bowls may be "nested' and the handles separated in a fanlike manner.

BELOW: The all-green floral decoration for this informal buffet harmonizes with the color of the chinaware, decorated with rural scenes. Strelitzia, dracena, clivia, arum leaves, and bells of Ireland are held in place by crumpled wire in a shallow bowl.

OPPOSITE: Regatta Day on a waterfront is exciting. A buffet for returning sailors is the most practical plan for a meal. A red, white, and blue nautical effect is created by the placement of the mats, napkins, and pottery. The large central hurricane lamp is filled with red peppers.

A cylindrical china pattern from Rosenthal, with medallion-like disk knobs and graceful handles. The decoration is in black and gold on white.

The fine white Wedgwood bone china set with black Basalt is in striking contrast to the orange mats and napkins.

Some of the most amusing parties can be held when friends come to help spruce up the house or decorate a new one. A door placed on trestles is one way of improvising a table for a buffet.

RIGHT: For informal meals in small apartments, the table can be set with all the dishes required for the service, including the dessert.

BELOW: Glass-top tables like this are practical on a porch or in a small dining area where heavier-looking tables may give a crowded look to the room.

OPPOSITE: An informal buffet with a black and white plaid cloth, red napkins, and red candles in a white Mexican candelabrum. The chafing dish and flatware are by Gorham.

TRAYS

Apart from being used to accommodate guests at a buffet dinner, tray tables are delightful adjuncts to informal family meals. They are also convenient by the fireside or for meals taken while watching a TV program. They are suitable too for invalids and for those who like a leisurely breakfast in a different setting. A cheese supper or snack meal is easily served in this manner. With cheese, crusty bread, crackers, or English biscuits, fresh fruit, red wine, and good coffee are the perfect accompaniments.

BARBECUES AND PICNICS

In the middle of the nineteenth century William Thompson, a Savannah, Georgia, newspaperman and fiction writer, recounted the adventures of a "Major Jones," who was staying in a hotel in Baltimore in the year 1843: ". . . and pretty soon after I got thar that everlastin' gong rung agin, and we all went in to dinner. I never seed sich a hundsum table in all my life before. It was long enuff for a fourth of July barbecue, and all dressed out like a weddin-supper."

This mention of a barbecue over a hundred and thirty years ago is interesting, for we are inclined to think of it as a fairly recent innovation. The barbecue is thoroughly American, but it has been adopted and adapted in other countries where the climate permits outdoor eating. A charcoal-cooked steak with salad is about as tempting an outdoor meal as can be devised, unless it is an old-fashioned American clambake at the shore. The barbecue is the delight of husbands who have longed for the masculine participation in the art of cookery long open to chefs but closed to mere husbands. These released inhibitions have raised the barbecue to gourmet status. The mechanics of a portable barbecue with rotisserie equipment is not for "the little woman" to worry about; it is he who takes care of the cooking, and perhaps may be equally happily employed tossing the salad while waiting for the steaks to be done. The hostess does the planning, sets the buffet table, is responsible for the decoration, prepares the vegetables and desserts, and greets the guests in a relaxed, proud-of-husband mood.

Barbecues are not only evening fare, but for midday picnics too — in the garden, by the lake, or on the beach. To some the barbecue is an art, to others a suburban mania, but nevertheless it has achieved popular status and makes summer entertaining easier and more pleasant for the whole family.

Pottery, earthenware, enamelware, hurricane lights, wooden and tole trays, basketry, stainless steel, copper, checkered linen, plastic mats, and, often, attractive paperware come into their own for this type of serve-yourself meal, where everybody helps.

PICNICS

One might perhaps think that picnics belong to the present century only, but they are a very old eating custom, as mentioned in Chapter 1, where an illustration shows Queen Elizabeth with her attendants enjoying a picnic in the forest. Today, these meals-on-the-move may be inspired by such activities as a sight-seeing drive through the country, camping expeditions, or a lake or beach party. Wherever the place, whatever the plan, a picnic should be gay in color and mood, and as simple in preparation and service as possible. However, for those who do not like to sit on the ground and want their creature comforts at a picnic, there are folding tables and chairs, and portable grills. Apart from the normal basic equipment necessary for the picnic fare your checklist might also include: a gay striped or checkered cloth with napkin-towels in matching or contrasting colors, paper or plastic cups and plates or enamelware in the same bright colors, a basket or carry-all for Thermos containers to keep drinks hot or cold, bottles of soft drinks or wine, and a smaller basket of fruit for easy handling.

Simplicity is the keynote for picnicking, but enjoying a beautiful day outdoors in a lovely natural setting can be done with a colorful flair if you have a mind for it. If one reviews the history of man's eating habits, it is perhaps not so strange that behind our civilized front the relaxed informality of the outdoor picnic — completely in contrast to a formal meal indoors — seems to make food taste better, especially if most of it may be eaten with the fingers.

OPPOSITE: On a beautiful day everything seems to taste better outdoors.

For a house with large windows an outdoor Christmas tree, planted and decorated, makes an enchanting backdrop for the holiday season. Here the table is set for eggnog and coffee. Wassail, punch, shandygaff, or switchel might replace the eggnog.

A sterling tea and coffee service made by the Gorham Company and presented to Mary Todd Lincoln, Abraham Lincoln's wife, by the people of New York City.

17.
Cocktail, Coffee,
and Other Parties

The cocktail party has several advantages, for both the hostess and the guest. It is informal, it normally has a time limit, and people can circulate and talk to the friends they most want to talk to, and many more guests can be accommodated than at a buffet or seated meal. At a small casual party for intimate friends the host or a man friend usually mixes the drinks. The food is customarily limited to snacks, dips, and appetizers which can be handled without messing the fingers. These are passed by the hostess at the beginning of the party and then placed conveniently for guests to help themselves.

For the larger party comprising people who may not know others, the host and hostess have to play a more active part; it is advisable, therefore, to have help at the bar if possible, and in the kitchen, too, if hot hors d'oeuvres are planned. The food, small in portion, should never be sweet; usually it is highly seasoned or is made up of such items as anchovies, sharp cheese, and olives. Good drinks, good food, compatible company, and sufficient room to circulate are the requisites for a good cocktail party.

For the really large affair, held when the main meal is eaten in the middle of the day and the guests may be coming some distance, a buffet is necessary. The menu can be simple, but hearty enough to substitute for a meal, with food that will keep fresh over the period of the party. A well-balanced plan would include one or more hot dishes, as well as cold meats, cheeses, relishes, a spread, and a variety of food that can be eaten with the fingers or with the aid of toothpicks. The food, with plates and napkins, and the cocktail equipment can be set on one table. But it is better to have the bar set up on a separate table with plenty of room for service, as guests usually like to drink for a while before eating. If you have a barman he can take orders and serve everything from the kitchen or pantry. Coffee should be ready in the kitchen, since it may be needed later in the evening.

COCKTAIL PARTY CHECKLIST

INVITATIONS. Mail or phone. The time is usually somewhere between 5 and 8 P.M. unless it is a come-when-you-can and stay-as-long-as-you-like buffet plan.

MUSIC. Some find this helpful as a background, particularly at the beginning of a party, but many people find it disturbing. Ashtrays should be large and plentiful. If arrangements can be made to have them emptied regularly, so much the better. For tables that do not have an alcohol-proof finish, a liberal supply of coasters should be available. Place small tables next to chairs so that guests can sit down with their drinks.

GLASSES. It is good to have on hand twice as many as your guest list.

ICE CUBES. Start freezing these at least a day ahead, to fill ice buckets, or else buy the cubes in quantity. Use only fresh ice for old ice absorbs tastes and odors.

FOOD. Many foods can be prepared well ahead and sealed in airtight wrapping for the refrigerator or freezer.

NAPKINS, SERVIETTES, AND HAND TOWELS. Have plenty of the gay paper cocktail napkins on the food and drink tables and an extra supply in reserve. Hand towels of soft absorbent paper, which seem to be preferred to dainty linen ones, should be well supplied in all bathrooms and powder rooms.

COCKTAILS. Follow a tested recipe and use a jigger for measuring, unless you are an expert guesser. Stir, rather than shake, all drinks made with clear liquors, such as martinis or Manhattans. Martinis can be made somewhat in advance and placed in a refrigerator. The ice is added later so that the cocktail is not diluted. Shake all cocktails that contain ingredients which are harder to blend, like daiquiris, Bloody Marys, and whisky sours. Prechill the glasses — this makes a big difference. Use lots of ice — but never twice. There is nothing worse than a lukewarm drink that was meant to be cold. For drinks like a Tom Collins, as a rule, sugar, fruit juice, and ice are put in the glass first, and then liquor is added. For a carbonated drink, like a gin and tonic, add ice, liquor, then the mix.

For those who do not like cocktails there are many alternatives, besides the traditional serving of whisky or sherry. Punch and eggnog are two favorites, and if you do not have your own recipes for these, any good liquor or wine shop will provide you with them. You might try a "cheese and wine" party, or make this a part of a cocktail party. Cheeses should be taken out of the refrigerator at least two hours beforehand as they should be enjoyed at room temperature, like the full-bodied red wine that is the perfect accompaniment.

The following are some drinks which may be enjoyed:

The Wine Cup

This is not a punch. In early days it was a communal cup and is still used as such in the annual feasts of the City of London. It is a compound of champagne, brandy or gin (vodka is sometimes used), and one or more sweet liqueurs, a charged water or sparkling wine, and, if desired, a sweetener. The garnish is composed of a rind of cucumber, thinly sliced, mint, fresh pineapple sticks, almost any berry (unstemmed for eating by hand after they have soaked in the cup), or spirals of lemon or orange peel. The wine cup may be prepared in advance and served in large brandy inhalers or champagne glasses.

The Wassail Bowl

This hot, spicy drink, which stems from medieval times, has become traditional at Christmas festivities. A modern, simplified version can be made as follows: poke cloves, $\frac{1}{4}''$ apart, into 3 oranges and bake for 30 minutes in a shallow pan. Heat 2 quarts of apple cider or apple juice until bubbles show around the edge. Remove, stir in $\frac{1}{2}$ cup lemon juice, and pour all ingredients into a heatproof punch bowl. Pierce 1 or 2 oranges with an ice pick in several places and place these in the bowl. Serve in mugs and use fragrant cinnamon sticks to stir. This recipe serves 10 or 12 people.

The Icy Shrub

This versatile nineteenth-century drink was a favorite of Thackeray. It can be mixed ahead in quantities and kept chilled in the refrigerator. For the basis of the "shrub" use the sweetened juice of any fruit and lace it with liquor (bourbon, rum, vodka, or gin), or with brandy or champagne. Use supplementary fruit liqueurs to intensify its fruit flavor. Garnish with mint sprigs, pineapple sticks, unstemmed cherries, peeled grapes, spirals of lime peel. Add chilled champagne or carbonated water to the individual highball glass at the last minute.

Here is a recipe for one kind of "shrub" that will serve 8 persons:

Santa Shrub

Blend 2 cups fresh orange juice (or one 12-ounce can undiluted frozen orange juice) strained, juice of 1 lemon or 2 limes, strained, 1 cup simple syrup, 1 cup Grand Marnier, $\frac{1}{2}$ cup orange-flower water, and 10 ounces vodka or light rum together, pour into large container, and refrigerate.

Shandygaff

This classic English drink is extremely easy to make. Pour equal quantities of ale and ginger beer over lots of ice. If you wish, add a dash of liqueur such as Grand Marnier or Cointreau. Serve immediately.

All of these drinks are suitably different to serve to those surprise visitors who drop in on New Year's Eve. In Scotland it is still customary for people to go "first-footing" on that

day. The first person to enter a house after midnight is known as a "first-foot" — a dark young man is preferred and he is supposed to bring a piece of coal. He is entitled to kiss whoever opens the door, whether mistletoe is hanging up or not. A first-footer should be toasted with something unusual. You might concoct a mint julep or do some research on Sherry Cobblers, Timber Doodles, and other rare drinks written about by Charles Dickens when he was staying in Boston, Massachusetts, in 1842.

The popular nineteenth-century harvest drink was "switchel." This consisted of 1 quart water, 1 tablespoon of sifted ginger, 3 heaping tablespoons of sugar, and 1 half-pint of vinegar. This healthy-sounding drink might appeal to the vinegar drinkers of today.

Early New Englanders used alcohol in various disguises, not only for celebrations but to quench the thirst resulting from eating salt meat and fish, and for a little internal heat-

ing in those cold houses warmed only by the hearth or stove. They enjoyed "hard" cider, a mixture of rum and cider known as "stone wall," a combination of rum and molasses called "blackstrap," and also a popular tavern drink known as "flip," which was rum with sugar and beer, heated with a red-hot poker. Ladies who would not dream of entering bars or taverns made elderberry and currant wine to share with their visitors.

In the last decade or so, coffee-and-dessert parties have become a simple way of entertaining close friends, especially for couples whose young families make a dinner party too much of a problem, except once in a while. They also fit into the scheme of things for people who like to see certain friends regularly for a game of bridge or to discuss projects of mutual interest.

The dessert for this informal plan can be as simple or as fancy as you wish, set on a pretty table with flowers and candles and a sweet wine or coffee to go with it.

In the sixteenth century desserts were served either as a separate meal or as a continuation of the main meal. In the seventeenth and eighteenth centuries a separate table was heavily laden with wet and dry fruits, ices, creams, jellies, syllabubs, and suckets. This table was then called an *ambique,* since the guests could wander around it, choosing whatever they wished.

Coffee may be served in various ways. You may like to serve a good strong coffee in a demitasse, or espresso with a twist of lemon. Another plan is to set an attractive tray with liqueurs, a little bowl heaped with whipped cream, cinnamon sticks to stir the coffee, and dishes filled with thin spirals of orange and lemon peel. Put the café filtre or espresso on the coffee tray with the small cups, pour the liqueur into the coffee and let the guests help themselves to whatever they wish.

For those who do not drink brandy, a white fruit liqueur such as kirsch or framboise, and crème de menthe are popular.

For certain gatherings men will prefer "a real cup of coffee and none of this fancy business" — to be followed by long drinks of hard liquor served by the host during the evening. In any event, the comfort and enjoyment of your guests is your primary consideration, and the simplicity of this kind of party is really its charm. If it is too elaborate, the purpose of it is defeated.

How was coffee discovered? It was first found in its wild state in Abyssinia, and from there it spread to Arabia, and was taken via the caravan route to India, Egypt, and Syria. One legend dating back to the third century tells of a herdsman who noticed that his goats became unusually lively after eating the berries of a certain shrub. When he tried them he, too, felt in a pleasant state of high spirits! The herdsman told the abbot of a monastery

OPPOSITE: Under a painting by Corot a charmingly decorated table provides serving space for coffee and liqueurs.

nearby about this discovery and he, finding it true, gave it to those brethren who often fell asleep during their nightly prayers.

In 800 A.D. coffee was used as food in parts of Africa, where it was ground between stones, mixed with grease, and rolled into balls. Later it became the custom to dry and roast the bean. Mohammedans took to drinking coffee instead of wine because they were told they would not go to Paradise otherwise.

From Arabia and Turkey its use soon spread to Europe. In the early seventeenth century, when Turkish invaders of Western Europe were driven out by the King of Poland, they left behind them large amounts of coffee. A Viennese procured enough to open a coffeehouse in Vienna, where he served it in the European style in which we use it today. From Vienna it was introduced to Rome by the middle of the seventeenth century, and thus Italy became one of the first countries on the Continent to claim it as a popular drink.

In 1650 the first coffeehouse was opened at Oxford, England, and it naturally became a meeting place for dons and students. Within a few years it was established in London and, in fact, within fifty years there were more than a thousand coffeehouses all over the city. These houses, which were a cross between a club and a tavern, were often known as "penny universities" because they attracted writers, artists, and other learned notables. Merchants also found them suitable places in which to transact business. One of the most famous was owned by Edward Lloyd, who used to list ships for the interest of the underwriters who came there. Later, it became Lloyd's Royal Exchange, and today it is the huge insurance business known all over the world as Lloyd's of London.

It was in these early coffeehouses that "tip" was coined. To speed the service, a box was put on the wall of the coffeehouse in which you dropped money intended for the waiter. This box was labeled "To Insure Promptness."

In London's British Museum there is a proclamation that closed the coffeehouses in 1675 (in the time of Charles II) because they were said to be used as meeting places for politicians and plotters who freely criticized the affairs of the country. It condemns ". . . divers false, malitious and scandalous reports to the defamation of His Majesty's government." It was withdrawn within ten days owing to the tremendous outcry it caused.

London had two thousand coffeehouses by the middle of the eighteenth century, and it is amusing to think that at this time tea — considered to be England's national drink — was more popular in America. Then, in 1767, George III laid duties on several export articles, including tea. When the British Parliament later repealed every tax except the one on tea, this caused the resentment that led to the famous Boston Tea Party of 1773. It was then that many patriotic colonists abandoned tea and turned to coffee. Today, England is the largest importer of tea, and America the largest importer of coffee.

OPPOSITE: Christmas wreaths on the table enhance a punchbowl. The wreaths used for both these buffet settings are made of fruit, evergreens, and dried materials.

The English silver tea service made in the 1800s and the delicate eight-eenth-century Limoges porcelain cups displayed in this beautifully furnished room are still used by the descendants of the original owner. The silver vase arranged with lilies is Louis XV, as are many of the other treasures.

A charming old pink and green Meissen tea set with a rose design.

18.
Tea – Its History and Meaning

The story of tea is as strange and as fascinating as any that one can read. A prehistoric event dating back some five thousand years is bound to be shrouded in many mysteries, but the exceptional qualities of tea are such that many legends developed concerning its beginnings. A highly civilized people like the Chinese considered it a special gift from heaven. In India, too, it was much the same. In Japan a special ceremony grew around it. This habit of drinking tea is the only purely Asian custom which commands universal interest. Through it the East and West have met — in a teacup! Its introduction had a charming influence on our Western culture, even though a great deal of smuggling and piracy helped to bring it about. Discriminating Chinese taste insisted that tea should be drunk from porcelain; and this subsequently had a tremendous effect on world trade and the voyages of clipper ships. Art, politics, and religion were all involved.

All this mystery and adventure stirred up many superstitions. Even today some tea companies attach a little saying to each teabag, such as:

"To stir tea in the pot is to stir up strife."

"Floating tea leaves mean 'watch for strangers coming.' To tell the gender and the day of arrival, put them on the back of one hand and tap with the back of the other until they adhere — each tap is one day — and if they are soft leaves it is a woman; if hard, a man."

Fortune-telling from tea leaves is not solely a gypsy custom. Many people have read meanings into the shapes and groups of leaves that form in the bottom of the cup — how accurately is, of course, another matter.

The philosophy of tea and tea cults, including Teaism, all express the association of man with nature. This association, according to one legend, began in the spring of the year 2737 B.C., with the Emperor Shen Nung, who was known also as the Divine Healer because of his interest in the medicinal qualities of herbs. While boiling his drinking water he was delighted by an unexpected aroma from the caldron, and on tasting the water he discovered the flavor to be astringent, clean, and refreshing. Some leaves from the branches of trees used as firewood had fallen into the pot.

This particular wood was gathered from the nearby camellia trees — that is, *Camellia sinensis*. (The Camellia is an Asiatic evergreen shrub or small tree of the family Theaceae; the common garden camellia is *Camellia japonica*.) The difference between a camellia and a tea plant is as great as many other botanical differences found in the large families of nature, but this difference was not well defined for centuries.

The tea plant started its journey through history by being prized first as a medicinal herb, with the virtues of "relieving fatigue, delighting the soul, strengthening the will, and repairing the eyesight." By the fifth century this native of southern China had become a food as well as a favorite beverage. Leaves were steamed and made into little cakes that were boiled with rice, ginger, orange peel, and onions. Today Tibetans living in primitive villages make this mixture into a syrup.

In the eighth century tea was celebrated in poetry and prose. The first book about tea, called *Ch'a Ching* or *Chaking* ("The Holy Scripture of Tea"), was written by Lu Yu. The author dealt comprehensively with every phase of tea consumption, from the growing of the plant to its final enjoyment, and he set forth a comprehensive "Code of Tea." One chapter covered every move in the ritual of proper drinking, and described the twenty-four instruments which formed the tea equipage. Later, Lu Yu understandably became the patron saint of the tea merchants.

Tea became more than a national drink — it became a part of religion, a way of life, and living proof to the Chinese that theirs was the only civilization and the rest of the world was barbaric.

The drinking of tea was now an art — and like all arts it had its periods and schools. The first was established by Lu Yu. This was the Classic period of the T'ang Dynasty (618-906) when cake tea was boiled. During the Romantic period, in the Sung Dynasty (960-1279), powdered tea was whipped in hot water by a delicate whisk made of split bamboo. The third school, known as the Natural period, came with the Ming Dynasty (1368-1644) and leaf tea or steeped tea prevailed. To this last school we today owe our understanding and appreciation of tea.

During the middle of this last period (about the fifteenth century) the cult of Teaism and the art of flower arrangement developed. Teaism, according to Okakura Kakuzo in his book, *The Book of Tea*, is the "art of concealing beauty that you may discover it, of suggesting what you dare not reveal. It is the noble secret of laughing at yourself, calmly yet thoroughly, and is thus humor itself—the smile of philosophy." Japan's long isolation from the rest of the world and the introspection that was prevalent during the fifteenth century made this a favorable time for the elevation of tea-drinking from a polite amusement to an aesthetic cult. Early Buddhist saints, so the legend goes, gathered the flowers strewn by the storm and, in their solicitude for all things, placed them in water and eventually gave them a subordinate part in the art of the tearoom.

The tea ceremony and flower arrangement have developed into separate arts, which have reached all levels of society. The great masters of each have contributed much to Japan's culture, revolutionizing the architecture and interior design of the Japanese home. They laid out all the most celebrated gardens, inspired the high quality of Japanese porcelain, and designed many exotic fabrics. Although many a Westerner feels that these arts make "much ado about nothing," through their study we can be made aware, as Okakura Kazuko said, of "the littleness of great things in themselves and the greatness of little things in others."

The formation of the Honourable East India Company was of greatest importance to the story of tea, for it was the biggest and most powerful monopolistic trading organization the world has known. In 1610 the Dutch brought the first tea to their homeland; it reached France in 1636, and Russia in 1638. In 1650 it arrived in England, where it was introduced as "that excellent and by all physicians approved China drink, called by the Chineans Tcha, and by other nations Tay, alias Tee," in an advertisement for tea in a newspaper, *Mercurius Politicus*.

In England it was at first treated as a pot herb—boiled, the water thrown away, and the leaves served with butter. However, by the beginning of the eighteenth century, tea was well on its way to capturing a second island race.

Tea was appreciated for its medicinal qualities, it is true, but primarily it was enjoyed as a delightful drink. It was said that tea "has not the arrogance of wine" and, according to the Emperor Shen Nung, it "is better than wine for it leadeth not to intoxication, neither does it cause a man to say foolish things and repent thereof in his sober moments. It is better than water for it does not carry disease; neither does it act like poison as water does when the wells contain foul and rotten matter."

The addition of milk came about 1680; whether it was to change the strength of the drink or to cool it for drinking is not really known, but it came to stay—in England, anyway.

At first tea was scarce and expensive and limited to the upper classes, who had the proper equipment for serving it and the time to spend enjoying it. Most of the paraphernalia was purely Western in design and usage, and has changed little today. Two articles,

ABOVE: A delightful little tea house in an American garden reproduces the charm of Japanese architecture. BELOW: Utensils for the tea ceremony (*cha-no-yu*), an aesthetic pastime in which powdered green tea is served, and appreciation of beauty in art and nature is cultivated. The Japanese ceremony is conducted according to the ancient and stylized custom. OPPOSITE: The tokonoma, an alcove found in traditional Japanese homes, is where guests are entertained.

the caddy and the cozy, remain particularly British. Because tea was expensive when first introduced, it was kept in a one-pound box called a caddy; the word is derived from the Malay *kati*, meaning a weight of approximately one pound.

Coffeehouses, already established in London in the early eighteenth century, were centers for political, social, and literary groups, where a man's drink accompanied masculine talk. A "dish of tea" could be had there, but tea seemed better suited to mixed company and the formality of afternoon social gatherings in private homes: "Tea without a lady to pour it is mere self-indulgence." Thackeray remarked, "Nature meant very kindly by women when she made the tea-plant," for the men went home instead of visiting the coffeehouses.

Tea-drinking spread to all classes with amazing rapidity. Visits to tea gardens in the country became the fashionable way to beguile a young lady on a pleasant afternoon.

Chinese unglazed stoneware, late seventeenth century.

French Vincennes porcelain, c. 1750.

Tea was introduced into Holland in 1610, into Russia in 1638, and into England in 1650. There it was presented as "that excellent and by all physicians approved China drink, called by the Chinese Tcha, and by other nations Tay, alias Tee." On these pages is a group of teapots from many parts of the world.

Venetian porcelain, c. 1725.

Chinese porcelain, reign of K'ang Hsi (1662-1722).

English Staffordshire stoneware, c. 1740.

French Sèvres porcelain, c. 1764.

English Leeds earthenware, c. 1775.

English Rockingham porcelain, c. 1840.

English Leeds earthenware tea-kettle and stand, late 1700s or early 1800s.

Japanese Sodeshi stoneware, c. 1930.

Afternoon tea in the sitting room of an old English house in Warwickshire.

In 1884 the first teashop opened in London, to be followed in the years to come by one on almost every street corner.

Food with afternoon tea was said to have been introduced in the early nineteenth century by Anna, wife of the Seventh Duke of Bedford, to avoid "that sinking feeling" while waiting for the late dinner hour. This later developed into the English high tea, still popular today in some areas.

England is the world's largest consumer of tea. The kettle is always "on the hob" ready for a "nice cup of tea" or "cuppa," as the phrase now goes, at any time of the day or evening. With some it is a "must" first thing in the morning as well as at breakfast, not to mention at teatime and last thing at night. Every man is entitled to his "elevenses" and his "four o'clocker" in the commercial world, and the teashops, many restaurants, and hotel lounges are geared for the general public's midafternoon halt in their affairs.

Tea is still the way of formally or informally entertaining those one wishes to spend a pleasant afternoon hour or so with. In the British Commonwealth and former colonies it is the same, particularly in Australia, where tea is the mainstay of the great "outback." The smoke-blackened billycan (made famous in the swagman's song "Waltzing Matilda") is ever ready for stewing a thirst-quenching "cuppa," morning, noon, and night.

Tea was first brought to America in the late seventeenth century. At that time cider, ale, and wine were the favorite table drinks, and the bitter concoction that New Englanders made with tea was enough to discourage anyone from adopting it. Few knew how to prepare it. Most often they boiled the leaves much too long, and then, after drinking the liquid, they salted the leaves and ate them with butter as had been done in England in the 1650s. After New Amsterdam passed into the hands of the English and became New York, it took on English customs, and tea, though still expensive, became more popular. At fashionable dinner parties the ladies withdrew after the meal was finished, and were rejoined later by the gentlemen in the parlor. Dessert in the form of fruit, biscuits, or cakes, was then served with tea. Tea was also taken privately in the morning and socially in the afternoon, following the English custom. In the homes of professional men tea was served with their earlier family supper.

And so drinking tea went hand in hand with the development of the private and social life of the eighteenth century. Acquiring the proper equipage and the etiquette for serving tea was the ambition of every housewife with social obligations. And even the very young used dolls' tea sets when they imitated grownups in the very serious world of make-believe. In either case everything was arranged in a very orderly manner, whether on a tray, a covered table, or even the bare wood. Teaspoons were placed in a pile or in a "spoon boat"; tea strainers rested on slop bowls. Tongs were used for lump sugar. Cream seems to have been preferred to milk; lemon, although apparently used earlier by Russians, appears not to have been used elsewhere in the West until the nineteenth century.

The earliest cups and teapots were small, because tea was expensive when first introduced. Later, tea services were made in several sizes. Originally the imported Chinese cups were without handles, but doubtless owing to the fact that tea was taken very hot, handles were added as a concession to foreign demand. The teapot was, of course, Oriental in design, since it was imported with the cargoes of tea. Once tea became a fashionable drink, and porcelain its accepted medium, tea services were made by every china factory in England and Europe — as well as in China.

Silver and pewter trays, teapots, sugarbowls, cream pitchers, teapot stands, and finally tea urns were all made to cater to the growing custom of tea-drinking. The tea urn — the last and most ornate form to be added to the expensive service — was actually for hot water. Canisters for the dry tea leaves were made of ceramic and silver and were often sold in sets of three in a chest or teacaddy. Some had dome-shaped tops for measuring the tea, otherwise caddy spoons or ladles were used.

Attending tea parties became as essential a part of the social round in New York, Philadelphia, and Boston as it was in London and all over England. The food served at these affairs included cakes and sometimes cold pastries, sweetmeats, preserved fruits, and plates of cracked nuts.

Guests were supposed to drink as much tea as possible to please their hostess and the only way they could indicate that they did not wish to imbibe further was to put a spoon across the cup.

Originally tea was exported mostly from China, but now it comes to Europe and America from India, which has become the world's largest exporter. The island of Ceylon is the second largest supplier to the world market.

There are more than three thousand varieties of tea and, like wines, they take their names from the districts where they are grown, such as Darjeeling, Assam, Ceylon, Java,

"An English Family at Tea" by an eighteenth-century Flemish artist. Handleless cups and a spoonboat are depicted.

etc. The tea in the markets today is a blend of twenty to thirty different varieties. Above 90 per cent of the tea we drink is the black variety, which comes from India, Ceylon, and Indonesia. Tea, like wine, should be drunk the way you like it, but its strength should never be judged by its color. Some weak teas produce a dark brew while some strong teas are light in color. Color and taste are also affected by the differences in water.

Good tea is simple to make but every detail is important if you want the best results: First warm the teapot by half filling it with hot water, then empty it and put in the tea leaves, a teaspoon for each cup and one "for the pot" if you like it strong. Pour on freshly boiled water and allow to steep. Three to five minutes is enough for the proper infusion.

The trick of making good tea lies in using boiling water at the right moment. Water that has been boiling for some time is flat and airless and has no action; the tea leaves will form a soggy ball at the bottom of the pot and scarcely move at all. On the other hand, water just below boiling point cannot extract all the ingredients from the leaves since the

OPPOSITE: The Governor's Palace, Williamsburg, Virginia, begun in 1720. The furnishings were largely English, as seen here in the small parlor, where a table is set with tea equipage. The colorful birds on the marble mantel are Chelsea.

leaves will simply rise to the surface and stay there. Cold water freshly drawn from the tap, then brought to the boil for a moment, is still full of air particles which help to activate the dried leaves before they settle, and thus the action of the air and the briskly boiling water extract the best flavor from the tea. The English saying, "bring the pot to the kettle, not the kettle to the pot," when the water boils, is a rule well worth following.

Tea experts have finally decided that milk, not cream, which was once popular, is the best addition to tea, for it lets the true flavor come through. Tea should be kept in a tightly covered container, away from spices and cooking odors. Always rinse the teapot after use, and never wash it with soap. Tea in bags, a practical American innovation early in this century, horrified our mothers and so distressed one Englishman that he wrote "Americans are no longer on intimate terms with tea." However, teabags have taken favor not only in the United States and Canada, but in England too, although tea never tastes as well when a tea bag floats in a pot or a cup. Instant tea and tea concentrate make the serving of a large gathering easier too, but cannot be expected to satisfy the true tea connoisseur's thirst, except in an iced drink. One-third of the tea drunk in America is iced, a concoction dating back to a hot summer day at the St. Louis World's Fair in 1904, when a tea merchant put ice in his tea, hoping it would cool him off. Twice as much tea is required for a glass of iced tea as for a cup. Made tea should never be put in the refrigerator, for it may become cloudy unless sugar or saccharine has been added.

LEFT: An ice-cold tea punch set in a buffet plan with watercress rolls is a simple way to entertain on a hot summer afternoon. OPPOSITE: An umbrella in a garden provides a cool setting for a tall glass of iced tea with a leisurely meal.

The following is an extract from *The Flowers Personified* by Grandville, published in an English translation in 1849:

The Coffee-flower took it into its head to make a voyage to China, for the purpose of visiting her sister, the Tea-flower. The latter received her guest with a politeness in which might be seen a slight air of superiority.

In fact, to the Tea-flower, Coffee was but an outside barbarian, with whom she condescended to hold intercourse, notwithstanding the immense distance that separates a civilized Chinese from a foreigner, who is still sunk in the depths of ignorance.

The Coffee-flower had too much quickness and penetration, not to understand this reception, and she had too much pride to submit to it. "My dear," said she to Tea, as soon as they were by themselves, "the airs which you affect, are not at all agreeable. Understand, if you please, that I do not need to be patronised, and that I am your superior in every respect."

The Tea-flower shrugged her shoulders with disdain. "My title of nobility," said she, "is six thousand years older than yours. It dates from the very foundation of the Chinese monarchy, the oldest of all known kingdoms."

"And what does that prove?" said Coffee.

"That you should treat me with deference," was the answer.

It is proper to state, that this conversation occurred at a small lacquered table, on which stood a coffee-pot and a tea-pot. The two flowers, to keep up their rage, had frequent recourse to the stimulants which these contained.

"You are so insipid," said Coffee, "that the Chinese themselves have been compelled to abandon you, and take to opium. You are no longer a stimulant, and a promoter of pleasant dreams — but merely a table-drink, like cider and small-beer among us."

"I have vanquished," quickly replied Tea, "a nation which has vanquished China itself. I reign in England."

"And I, in France."

"It was I that inspired Walter Scott and Lord Byron!"

"I nerved the wit of Molière and Voltaire."

"You are only a slow poison."

"And you, a mere vulgar diet-drink."

"In the melodious murmurs of the tea-kettle," said Tea, "one may fancy that he hears the spirits of the fireside sing. My color is that of a fair girl's tresses. I am the poesy of the gentle and melancholy north."

"Mine," said the Coffee-flower, "is the dusky tint of tropical maidens. Like them, I am ardent. Like some subtile fire, I course along the veins. I am the Cupid of the south."

"Thou dost consume, while I comfort."

"No — I give strength; you only weaken."

"To me belongs the heart."

"Yes; and to me the head."

The tea and coffee flowers consuming their favorite brews. Nineteenth-century engraving.

The two flowers had become so exasperated, that they were about to pull each other's leaves. But, on further reflection, they concluded to refer their dispute to a tribunal composed equally of tea-drinkers and coffee-drinkers. This tribunal has been long in session, but has not yet agreed on a verdict.

Children love bobbing for apples, whether the fruit is floating in a tub or suspended on strings, as here. The gay cloth and napkins are homemade, and the utensils are old-fashioned enamelware.

19.
Parties for Children and Teen-agers

Since children and teen-agers have such different tastes and interests, it is usually better to hold separate parties for the two age groups. While raising my family, I have given innumerable children's parties, and sponsored many teen-ager gatherings. Here are a few suggestions based on the most successful ones.

CHILDREN'S PARTIES

These, of course, should preferably be held in the daytime — and it is far better to have a short, happy party than a long-drawn-out struggle. I always preferred to have a party for children between meals so that the food served may be special, rather than what they normally eat. Usually the very young are too excited — or too shy — to eat much anyway, and their normal healthy appetites are renewed before the regular mealtime. A word of advice — insist that mothers collect their children at an appointed time, for the young have party hangovers, too.

It is no use being a nervous mother, expecting perfection from your child or the guests. Instead, try to enjoy whatever happens and the chances are that you will find children's parties a lot of fun, even if they are exhausting.

Gentle reminders to the young host or hostess of what he should do may lead him to do the right thing, and feel proud that he did — rigid rules make most children go into reverse gear.

Children seem to like to make their own fun; parties that are elaborate and too well organized bore them. Little boys are bored at little girls' parties. I find that the sexes are best entertained separately at this age. The girls like to show off their pretty dresses while they work out Valentine favors, paint Easter eggs, make or fix things to put on the Christmas tree, and do other "sissy" things. My greatest success was achieved by setting up a folding table with long benches either side in the playroom, making a sample butterfly-type decoration, and giving each child the ingredients (pipe cleaners, beads, different scraps of colored felt, glue, wire, and sequins, etc.) to make the same thing for herself. Out of ten guests no two made butterflies alike. I learned more than the children and had as much fun as they did, and one and a half hours went by like a puff of wind.

Little boys, on the other hand, prefer (if you ask them) to wear blue jeans and sneakers and have a picnic or some outdoor affair which might get a little rough. They like to make things too — but with scraps of wood, a knife, and other more dangerous tools. If the party has to be mixed, a trip to the zoo or a picnic in the garden, woods, or at the beach could be a real treat. In America, Halloween is a good time for the mixed party too, for both sexes are interested in getting dressed up and going the rounds for their "trick or treat." As the time spent waiting for the sun to go down seems like eternity to them, an afternoon party or supper allows them to get dressed early and start the fun earlier so that bedtime is more acceptable.

Birthday parties are the most popular in every country, chiefly because the young host or hostess gets presents, and games are usually planned, and the eating of a birthday cake is a special treat. Children will tell you ahead of time what games they like to play. To keep six or more youngsters going on one idea for long is impossible, for they lose interest quickly if they are not all participating to the same extent. Thus many changes of plan have to be thought of in advance.

Expensive decorations are wasted on children. They like color, and ideas that are related to their interests. A balloon — usually to pop — means more to them than a basket of flowers. The grown-up hostess has the responsibility of seeing that all the guests have a good time, so it is wise to keep the young guests down to a controllable number.

Food is rarely a problem, with a cake or ice cream — or both — heading the list in popularity. Individual cakes, in paper cups for easy handling and decorated with some removable nonsense such as candy flags or little faces made of round nuts and decorations, appeal to the eye as well as to the tummy, and can be counted on to keep the children occupied for a few precious minutes. Small sandwiches that are different from everyday fare, and other finger foods, are always better things to serve than dishes requiring utensils.

Each guest likes to take home something — a small toy, a balloon, some garlands or streamers, English crackers that go bang when they are pulled and contain a toy or paper hat, or lollipops or taffy apples on a stick. A basement or playroom — or outdoors — is ideal for children's parties, especially at Eastertime, when searches for hidden eggs can cause a shambles in the living room or dining room. There must, of course, be room for the young to run about — you are doomed to failure if you expect them to sit still for long.

TEEN-AGERS ENTERTAIN

The age group is important, for what is "hip" to a thirteen-year-old is "passé" to a fourteen-year-old and positively "out" to a fifteen-year-old. Beyond that age group only a genius can expect to cope.

Don't "do" for your teen-agers. Help with ideas, make suggestions from experience, and, within reason, let them make final decisions. Give encouragement (for your personal approval should be important) and — if you want your children to continue to bring their friends home — find something to congratulate them on, no matter what the results. Whatever they do themselves means more to them than anything magnificent you can concoct, even with great effort and expense. My experience has been that they do not like to spend a lot of money, but prefer to keep the cost of a party within the range of their allowances and therefore within the range of their values. My own teen-agers and their friends used a "share plan." They did things together — the more the merrier, and the more noise the better. Each young guest has a talent he is dying to show off; it is your job to discover it and suggest how it can best be used.

For a group of ten teen-agers, their plan might be something like this:

1. Can cook — so the menu is planned within the range of that person's abilities and experience.

2. Is interested in cooking — becomes assistant chef.

3. Can decorate, has a color sense. May dye an old sheet for a table cover, or make amusing cut-outs for wall decoration. Knows where to get gay posters, etc.

4. Has a father with a work shop — is appointed decorating assistant.

5. Can play a guitar or some other instrument, or has the best selection of records.

6. Has a radio to plug into an outlet for a pool party when the guitar player rests, or the visitors tire of records.

7. Good organizer — calls the gang (to relieve the line at the house of the hostess). Is the central office for the handling of problems, requests for help, any cancellations or changes. Has three helpers, as follows:

8. General secretary — not very good at arithmetic but his or her father has an adding

OPPOSITE: For Easter blown eggs are hung on gilded branches and the base is covered with dried tree fungi.

A Halloween supper table with decorations in keeping with the "high spirits" of the occasion.

machine, which is fun to use. Collects all dues if it is a group party — ahead of the party — in cash (no promises or penknives).

9. Has a brother who is allowed to drive the family car, and has permission to use the brother and his car for necessary shopping, and for picking up the members of the gang who do not have transportation.

10. Mop-up chief — responsible for seeing that all paperware used is put tidily in garbage cans, and that the party area is left in A1 condition.

Teen-agers, of course, prefer evening parties, to which both sexes are invited, and make their own plans for entertainment. Their food plans are more normal. They under-

stand parental supervision but want it to be felt rather than seen. Contrary to parents' fondest hopes, they do not care to dress up — informality is the keynote. In the late teens dancing is more popular than games, and buffets are the easiest plans for food arrangement. I have always found that small parties with good talk and good music, where punch and sandwiches were served, were enjoyed by certain groups of young people. And I might as well say that I know I am old-fashioned (in their eyes) but I insist that invitations, once accepted, must not be ignored if something better turns up, that the home is not a hotel, and that good manners are not prehistoric and quaint. I admit that youngsters may have a changing set of values, but certain values do not change.

The pleasure and knowledge to be gained by furnishing a doll's house, especially an old one, are not to be minimized. The fascination of things in miniature draws attention to detail, which is invaluable in furnishing full-size rooms. The dining room (ABOVE) measures thirteen inches high by eighteen inches wide. The tiny handleless cups on the table (RIGHT) are antique copies of early Worcester.

RIGHT: American teen-agers love to entertain high-school "grid-iron" heroes, and they prefer to make their own plans for entertainment and decoration. For this party, chocolate rice is molded into football shapes.

OPPOSITE: For a small dinner party to honor a classmate, the table is set with Wellesley College service plates in Wedgwood "Queensware" and heirloom sterling. The cloth is cornflower-blue Belgian linen by Matouk.

BELOW: A scooped-out watermelon is an ideal container for summer punch.

Blue and white Ming bowl decorated with pine, prunus, and bamboo.

20.
Check List

Date

Far enough ahead so that you can be fairly sure that the guests on your selected list can come. Choose a day that you know is likely to be most convenient for everyone. Be sure that this does not conflict with any major event scheduled ahead for any member of the family or with a national holiday.

Invitations

Whether given by phone or by mail, these should be explicit about directions and should indicate what is to be worn for the evening.

Be prepared to greet your guests on arrival, and later to give them a personal farewell. Successful parties take clever, detailed organizing, but once the "show is on the road" relax, so that your guests feel that everything is so smooth it just happens naturally.

OPPOSITE: A setting in muted colors with Japanese lacquer soup bowls on "pearl" place mats. The silver is Gorham's "Buckingham" and the crystal is "State Plain."

Menu

Plan the kind of food you do best, that is commonly acceptable to the majority of people and is easiest to serve. If you have to be reckless or inspired, save your ideas for the dessert. Complicated and unusual dishes are for the experienced cook, and a jumping-jack hostess makes everyone nervous.

Service

Start training your family early to do the necessary jobs that they can do as well as you can. If they do them regularly they should not feel imposed upon for this extra effort. Every member can help and everyone will help if it is understood beforehand, and not a last-minute request. Do not invite more than your table will hold conveniently, with plenty of room for service.

A resident maid usually has a full schedule and a dinner party is extra work. Therefore compensation should be considered, or extra help hired. Thoughtful consideration works wonders.

Make a List

In fact, make several lists. No one's memory is infallible. Begin with a shopping list from your menu; add anything you are running short of in the house that might be needed at the last minute, such as spray starch for table linen, and paper towels for the kitchen. Check essentials such as salt, whole peppers for the grinder, herbs, and sugar. Include parsley or watercress for decorating the dishes — for looks count as well as taste. For the smokers, add cigarettes and matches. Also add candles that are tall enough to be above eye level when in holders, guest hand towels in attractive absorbent paper, and all bar supplies. A wise hostess deals regularly with a good butcher, for only the French housewife is adept at treating poor meat.

A Countdown for Dinner Day

Two Days Before   Check platters and serving pieces against the menu — also glasses in case you have to borrow some.

Order flowers if you need special varieties, and have them delivered early on the day of the party.

If you have no hot plate, borrow one, or plan an area away from the activities around the stove where something can be set up for warming dinner plates and serving platters.

Check and press linen, and check silver for polishing. Wash seldom-used glassware and serving platters. Set up written timetable for food preparation on the day of the event.

One Day Before   Clear the refrigerator to make as much room as possible. Do shopping. Clean salad greens, fix frozen desserts, cheese pies or molds, and any other part of your menu that can be done ahead of time.

Do basic housecleaning. There is no time to worry about the woodwork.

Set candles firmly in all holders with florist's clay.

256

THE DAY OF THE PARTY   Soak flowers in deep water on arrival from the florist or after picking them from the garden. At least two hours should be allowed for them to harden.

Fill ice buckets with extra cubes.

Check the house for last-minute details — do the final dusting, place large ashtrays and cigarettes throughout party rooms, and a pile of hand towels in all bathrooms. Clear the coat closet for guests' apparel. Make a place for boots and umbrellas if necessary.

Set the table, and arrange flowers and centerpiece.

Complete the food preparations as planned.

Set up the bar.

Allow time for everyone to be dressed and relaxed before the guests are expected.

Make a final check with the family, the maid, or hired help on what is expected of them.

WHAT EVERY HOSTESS SHOULD HAVE

1. Her own party cookbook or workbooks, tried and tested.
2. Several bridge tables.
3. Folding chairs that are comfortable and can be stacked away in the basement or attic.
4. Shelves in the basement, attic, or storage room where party supplies can be stacked.
5. Colored cardboard to cut into strips — two of each color for each man guest, one for his hat and one for the top pocket of his coat. At large parties this will be a real help to departing guests.
6. A two-tiered serving cart on wheels (better than another pair of feet!)
7. Plain, uncolored Christmas lights, to make a patio or small garden into a fairyland.
8. Enough matching silver for her party needs. Every fall and winter many silver manufacturers authorize dealers to take orders for inactive patterns for delivery the following July.
9. Small guest soaps for individual use.
10. Powder-room supplies, including tissues, ashtrays, and new combs.
11. Trays in all sizes, shapes, and materials.
12. Several cans of air-fresheners for use in the playroom or den after heavy smokers.
13. A way with flowers. Not dotted everywhere, but arranged in one or two places in the living room, as well as on the dining table. Their gay color will complement your decor and give a real "lift" to the party.
14. A way with music — the right kind, the right tone.
15. An up-to-date record of your china and glassware, so that last-minute counting

can be avoided. If you must mix your china and silverware, alternate them around the table so that the over-all effect is not spotty.

16. One or two people to call on for special help when entertaining.

17. A good selection of cheeses and a plan for their service, as an alternative to the dessert offered.

18. Some soft drinks on hand for guests who do not drink hard liquor or wine.

19. Large wine glasses for the do-it-yourself dinner party. Use the 10-ounce size even for white wine, so that the host has to serve only once during a course.

20. Good conversation.

Contemporary silver, china, and glass set in a modern apartment. The sterling is "Esprit" by Gorham and the china is the "Swirl" pattern by Lenox.

OPPOSITE: The value of color is emphasized excitingly by these cobalt-blue and green glasses against a collection of pewter brought from Peking.

A Philadelphia mahogany tea-table.

Appendix

Many phrases which we use today have culinary connections, and the origins of some of them are given below. Also included are some data on our playing cards.

The Ceremonial Salt

In the banqueting hall of the baronial castle, the nobility sat at the head of the great T-shaped table with the Lord and Master, while the first cousins, second cousins, and so on, dwindled into the distance down the table. At the point of demarcation which set apart the landed gentry from the common serfs was placed a "great standing salt," or "ceremonial salt." It was passed from here up the table; if you sat below the salt you were not only "not worth your salt" but you did not get any.

Upper Crust

The expression "upper crust" comes from the same era, when the great crusted meat pies were served from the top of the table on down. Obviously the "gentry" got first choice of the crisp, flaky upper crust, and those at the foot of the table were more apt to get the soggy under crust.

Best Bib and Tucker

When one dresses in his finest clothes, he is said to put on his best bib and tucker. This term originated in the late seventeenth century. The bib, not unlike a child's bib today, served to keep men's clothes clean while they were eating. The tucker, usually lace or muslin, was tucked into the necks of women's dresses. Thus a couple dressed in the best bib (the man) and tucker (the woman) were all decked out for a fancy dinner party.

OPPOSITE: This green-bordered dinner service was made at the Royal Worcester Porcelain Factory between 1813 and 1840, when the company was known as Flight, Barr and Barr. Family silver, Venetian wine glasses and decanters, and green German glasses mix harmoniously with American table linen.

Welsh Rabbit

Welsh "rabbit" is amusing and correct — and Welsh "rarebit" is wrong. This misconception, spread by restaurant menu writers, is, unfortunately, widely accepted. The true phrase dates back almost to Shakespeare's time. In those days only the wealthy could afford game from the royal preserves in Wales. Since rabbit itself was in scarce supply "Welsh rabbit" was the term adopted for melted cheese on toast.

In similar fashion, scrambled eggs on toast spread with anchovy butter came to be known as "Scotch woodcock." In New England codfish is sometimes called "Cape Cod turkey."

No Tea in Him

A man with "no tea in him," in the common parlance of the Japanese during the development of Teaism, was one "insusceptible to the seriocomic interests of the personal drama." "He's not my cup of tea" or "my dish of tea" are well-known phrases applied to those we do not care for.

A Pretty Kettle of Fish

This odd phrase came from a custom common along the Scottish border. At the start of the annual salmon run, large groups congregated for picnics along the banks of the streams. The salmon was boiled in huge pots and eaten in the hands. The disorder and mess which resulted came to be known as a "pretty kettle of fish."

Drink a Toast

The pleasant and civilized custom of drinking a toast to the good health of a friend began in ancient times. In Shakespeare's time, a piece of toasted bread was put in the tankard before ale or wine was poured in, to improve the taste, and to collect sediment and impurities at the bottom of the vessel. Thus the drink became a toast. The "toast of the town" is one whose great popularity causes many to drink his health.

The usual custom in those days was to pour a little of the wine into the host's glass, and some into the guest's, before either drank. Few trusted anyone outside the family circle and this was the only way to be sure the host had not poisoned your drink. Later, the ceremonial clicking of glasses was accompanied with the spoken wish, "To your good health."

Apple-Pie Order

One derivation of the phrase "apple-pie order" is thought to be a corruption of the French term *nappe plié*, meaning "folded linen." The term was commonly used in England long before it appeared in America. A New England theory is that it comes to us from a Colonial housewife who baked her pies ahead for the week to come and placed them in order on the shelf, thus giving rise to the phrase.

To Bring Home the Bacon

A noblewoman in Dunmow, England, decreed that "any person from any part of England going to Dunmow and humbly kneeling on two stones at the church door may

A French pastry shop in the seventeenth century. The pies and cakes for sale are spread out on a cloth folded and creased in small squares as was customary at that time. An engraving by Abraham Bosse.

claim a gammon of bacon, if he can swear that for twelve months and a day he has never had a household brawl or wished himself unmarried." This happened in 1111 A.D., and only eight persons won their side of bacon in the next five centuries. But the phrase also refers to the greased-pig contest at country fairs where the winner brings home the bacon.

Beer and Skittles

A mug of beer and a friendly game of skittles (the old-fashioned game of ninepins using a flattened disk to hurl at the pins) was the average British yeoman's idea of paradise in centuries past.

Drunk as a Lord

"Two- and three-bottle men" were not unusual among leaders in society during the reign of George III of England. Intoxication was the mark of a gentleman, and to be "drunk as a lord" was to be very drunk indeed: sometimes even to the extent of collapsing under the table.

Neither Fish nor Fowl nor Good Red Herring

In the Middle Ages the three chief classes other than the nobility were the clergy, lay people in general, and paupers. Fish was considered suitable for the clergy, while the common people ate fowl and the very poor were lucky to get red herring. Therefore something that was neither fish nor fowl nor good red herring was hardly suitable for anyone. Today the phrase is applied to a plan or idea that is vague and usually worthless.

Humble Pie

In England this "pie" was made from "umbles" — the heart, liver, and gizzard of a deer. When the huntsmen brought back the kill, the lord of the manor and his guests feasted on venison and the huntsmen and the servants, being of inferior rank, had, of necessity, to be satisfied with humble pie.

Salad Days

Shakespeare in *Antony and Cleopatra* wrote, "My salad days, when I was green in judgment, cold in blood." Thus Cleopatra described youth, with its lack of experience and maturity, and today oldsters apply the phrase "salad days" to the days of youth which appear "green" to their eyes.

Talk Turkey

To talk turkey means to talk serious business, and it was indeed serious "turkey talk" in the early Colonial days, so the story goes. A white man and a friendly Indian decided to share whatever the day's hunt brought them. They bagged three crows and two turkeys. The white man divided the birds by giving a crow to the Indian and a turkey to himself. When this happened again, it is said that the Indian complained, "You talk all turkey for you. Only talk crow for Indian."

THE STORY BEHIND OUR PLAYING CARDS

Bridge luncheons, teas, and dessert evenings planned around a game of cards may be more interesting if you realize that the cards have changed little since they first appeared some six hundred years ago. The kings, queens, and jacks dressed in handsome medieval robes, with their ancient symbols of authority, were legendary or Biblical heroes and heroines. The four suits represented the estates or ranks of society as they were in the Middle Ages:

Hearts represented courage and the highest development of humanity and were thus assigned to churchmen.

Spades (from the Spanish word *espada*, meaning "sword") represented the soldier.

Diamonds stood for wealthy merchants who traded in precious things.

Clubs represented the peasants and farmers.

The word "trumps" is simply a short form of "triumph," for in trumping, your card triumphs over cards of other suits.

The joker, often a very decorative card, is the oldest of them all; it came from the tarot pack still used by gypsies for fortune-telling.

The kings, representing the four great monarchies of the Middle Ages, are as follows:

King of spades — David, ruler of Israel, who overcame Goliath.

King of clubs — Alexander the Great. The only one shown with an orb, the symbol of his world empire.

King of diamonds — Julius Caesar. The one shown with a battle axe — the other three have swords.

King of hearts — Charlemagne, who refounded the Roman Empire in 800 A.D. The only one without a mustache.

The queens are not the wives of their respective kings but are as follows:

Queen of spades — Athena, the Greek goddess of war and wisdom. The only one shown with a royal scepter as well as the flower the other queens hold.

Queen of clubs — usually identified with Elizabeth I of England, known as "Good Queen Bess."

Queen of diamonds — Rachel, the Biblical heroine for whom Jacob toiled fourteen long years.

Queen of hearts — Judith, who, according to the Bible, proved her courage by cutting off a general's head.

The two knaves without mustaches were Knights of the Round Table:

Jack of clubs — Sir Lancelot of the Lake.

Jack of Diamonds — Sir Lancelot's half-brother, Sir Hector.

Jack of spades — Hogier the Dane, a cousin of Charlemagne.

Jack of hearts — La Hire, a famous French warrior who fought with Joan of Arc.

An eighteenth-century illustration showing a knot in the corner of the tablecloth — perhaps to weigh it down and hold it in place or to shorten its length and keep it out of the way of the young man on the left. Engraving by N. de Launay after Jean Michel Moreau, le Jeune.

Bibliography

American Heritage Cookbook and Illustrated History of American Eating and Drinking. New York, 1964.

Boggs, Kate Doggett. "A Glimpse of Old Table Settings." *Antiques,* vol. 26 (September 1934).

Byrd, Elizabeth. *Immortal Queen.* New York, 1965.

Clair, Colin. *Kitchen and Table.* New York, 1965.

Comité Interprofessionnel du vin de Champagne. *The Champagne Wine.* Epernay, France.

Cooper, Charles. *The English Table in History and Literature.* London, 1944.

Corning Museum of Glass. *Glass from the Corning Museum of Glass.* Corning, N.Y., 1958.

Cummings, Abbot Lowell. *Rural Household Inventories 1675–1775.* Boston, 1964.

Cummings, Richard Osborn. *The American and His Food: A History of Food Habits in the United States.* Rev. ed. Chicago, 1941.

Dow, George F. *Domestic Life in New England in the 17th Century.* Tuffsfield, Mass., 1925.

Elville, E. M. *The Collector's Dictionary of Glass.* London, 1961.

Felton, R. F. *British Floral Decoration.* London, 1910.

Garvin, Fernande. *French Wines.* New York, 1963.

Glasse, Hannah, *The Compleat Confectioner...* London, c. 1760.

Godden, Geoffrey A. *An Illustrated Encyclopaedia of British Pottery and Porcelain.* New York, 1966.

Grandville. *Les Fleurs Animées.* Translated by N. Cleaveland. New York, 1849.

Gurney, Gene. *The Smithsonian Institution.* New York, 1964.

Hampson, Simpson, and Norman, John Frederick. *The English at Table.* London, 1944.

Haynes, E. Barrington. *Glass through the Ages.* Rev. ed. Baltimore, Md., 1959.

Hill-Bigelow, Francis. *A History of Silver of the Colonies and Its Makers.* New York, 1917.

Himsworth, J. B. *The Story of Cutlery; from Flint to Stainless Steel.* London, 1953.

Hole, Christina. *The English Housewife in the Seventeenth Century.* London, 1953.

Honey, W. B. *Old English Porcelain.* New York, 1928.

——. *German Porcelain.* New York, 1946.

——. *Dresden China.* New York, 1947.

——. *English Pottery and Porcelain.* London, 1947.

——. *European Ceramic Art* (2 vols.). London, 1949.

——. *Wedgwood Ware.* New York, 1949.

——. *French Porcelain of the 18th Century.* London, 1950.

Horticulturalist and Journal of Rural Art and Rural Taste, The. New York, 1871.

Hughes, George B. *English, Scottish and Irish Table Glass.* New York, 1956.

——, and Hughes, Therle. *Three Centuries of English Domestic Silver.* London, 1952.

Iverson, Marion Day. "Table Linen in Colonial America." *Antiques,* vol. 76 (November 1959).

Lane, Arthur. *Italian Porcelain.* New York, 1954.

Larousse Gastronomique; the Encyclopaedia of Food, Wine and Cookery. English translation. New York, 1961.

Markham, Gervase. *English Hus-wife...* London, 1615.

McKearin, Helen. "Sweetmeats in Splendor: Eighteenth-Century Desserts and their Dressing Out." *Antiques,* vol. 67 (March 1955).

McKearin, Helen and George S. *American Glass.* New York, 1950.

——. *Two Hundred Years of American Blown Glass.* New York, 1941.

Miller, Roy Andrew. *Japanese Ceramics.* Tokyo, 1960.

Morris, Joan. *The ABC of Collecting Chinaware.* New York, 1960.

Morris, William and Mary. *Dictionary of Word and Phrase Origins.* New York, 1962.

Mudge, Jean McLure. *Early American Table Settings 1600–1850.* Winterthur, Dela., 1957.

——. *Chinese Export Porcelain for the American Trade.* Wilmington, Dela., 1962.

Okakura Kakuzo. *The Book of Tea.* Rutland, Vt., 1964.

Oman, Charles. *English Domestic Silver.* London, 1962.

Palmer, Arnold. *Movable Feasts. A Reconnaissance of the Origins and Consequences of Fluctuations in Meal-Times* ... New York, 1953.

Pepys, Samuel. *Diary* (2 vols.). New York, 1946.

Price, Pamela Vandyke. "The Pursuit of Rare Meats." *Tatler,* London (November 1964).

Rackham, Bernard. *Book of Porcelain.* London, 1910.

———. *The Glaisher Collection of Pottery and Porcelain.* Cambridge, England, 1935.

———. *Early Staffordshire Pottery.* London, 1948.

———. *Italian Majolica.* London, 1952.

Roth, Rodris. *Tea Drinking in 18th-Century America: Its Etiquette and Equipage.* United States National Museum Bulletin 225. Smithsonian Institution, Washington, D.C., 1961.

Schlesinger, Arthur. *Learning How to Behave.* New York, 1946.

Schoonmaker, Frank. *Encyclopedia of Wine.* New York, 1964.

Scott, J. M. *The Great Tea Venture.* New York, 1965.

Sedgwick, Catharine. *Morals of Manners.* New York, 1846.

Seranne, Ann, and Tebbel, John. *The Epicure's Companion.* New York, 1962.

Sprackling, Helen. *Customs on the Table Top.* Sturbridge, Mass., 1958.

———. *Courtesy: a Book of Modern Manners,* New York, 1947.

Street, Julian. *Table Topics.* New York, 1959.

Taylor, Gerald. *Silver.* Rev. ed. Baltimore, Md., 1956.

Thorpe, W. A. *English Glass.* London, 1961.

Vavra, Jaroslav R. *5,000 Years of Glass.* English translation. Prague, 1954.

Victoria and Albert Museum. *Teapots.* 1955.

———. *British Pewter.* 1960.

———. *Tables,* by J. F. Hayward, 1961.

———. *Cream-coloured Earthenware.* 1961.

———. *English Cutlery,* by J. F. Hayward. 1961.

Wason, Betty. *Cooks, Gluttons and Gourmets: A History of Cookery.* New York, 1962.

Whitehill, Jane. *Food, Drink and Recipes of Early New England.* Sturbridge, Mass., 1963.

Wilson, Kenneth M. *Glass in New England.* Sturbridge, Mass., 1959.

Wilson, Margery. *Pocket Book of Etiquette.* New York, 1937.

Acknowledgments

My sincere gratitude is extended to the following people for their interest and help: Mme. Philippe Bardet for research and for providing flowers in Switzerland; Miss Paola Bruscoli for research in Italy; Mrs. Martha Cronly for supervising the photography at the Wickham-Valentine House (the Valentine Museum), Virginia; Miss Virginia Daiker, Reference Librarian, Library of Congress, Washington; Miss Ann Dowzard for research and editorial help; Dr. Morrell Draper for research in England; Miss Marion Day Iverson and *Antiques* magazine for use of material in "Table Linen in Colonial America"; Mrs. Joan Morris for porcelain research; Mrs. Jean McClure Mudge for use of material in her research paper *Early American Table Settings 1600-1850;* Mr. Paul Quintus, Agricultural Attaché, United States Department of Agriculture, Paris; Mrs. Olive Reid for general assistance in preparations for photographing table settings; and Mr. Bryan Holme of Studio Books for his never-ending help and encouragement.

I am indebted to many people for allowing me to set tables and take photographs in their homes, and their names appear in the following list. In addition I would like to thank all the firms who kindly supplied me with pictures and material for the book, and their names are credited below:

Illustration credits
(Page numbers are given in parentheses)

All color photographs were taken by Louis G. Beaugrand except where otherwise indicated.

Chapter 1. (8) Bettmann Archive, New York. (9) The Louvre. (10) Rapho Guillumette, New York. (12, 13) National Gallery, London. (14) British Museum. (15) Top: Alinari Art Reference Bureau. Bottom: Piazzale degli Uffizi, Florence. (16) Top: The Metropolitan Museum of Art. Bequest of James C. McGuire, 1931. Center and bottom: British Museum. (17) Musée Condé, Chantilly. Photo: Giraudon, Paris. (18) British Museum. (19) Top: Woodcut from Turberville's *Book of Hunting,* 1575. Radio Times Hulton Picture Library, London. Bottom: Biblioteca Marciana, Venice. (20) Top: Radio Times Hulton Picture Library, London. Bottom: The Wallace Collection, London. (21) Top: Victoria and Albert Museum. Bottom: British Museum. (22) Top: German National Museum, Nuremberg. Bottom: Collection of Mr. Rockwell Gardiner. Photo: Louis Beaugrand. (23) Musée Condé. Photo: Giraudon. (24) Victoria and Albert Museum. (25) Museum of Fine Arts, Boston. (26) Top: Victoria and Albert Museum. Bottom: Valentine Museum, Richmond, Va. (27) Museum of Fine Arts, Boston. (29) Painting dated 1946. Galerie St. Etienne, New York.

Chapter 2. (30) Table setting by Contessa Bossi-Pucci Serristori at Palazzo Strozzi. Photo: Fototeca Azienda Autonoma di Turismo. (31) Collection of Mr. Jack Levsky. (32) Top: Tiffany & Co. Bottom: Tea Council, New York. (33) Mr. and Mrs. Rockwell Gardiner's house, Connecticut. Photo: Louis Beaugrand. (35) Mr. and Mrs. Louis Dreyfus's house, New York. (36) Mrs. Anne Valentine Cesare's house, Connecticut. (37) Table setting by Princess Chumbhot, Bangkok. Bottom: The Chumbhot and Pantip Collection. (38) Top and bottom: Tiffany & Co. (39) Top: Ginori. Bottom: Mr. and Mrs. Cyril Jewsbury's house, England. Photo: Lacy's Studio, England. (40) Top: American Sweden News Exchange. Bottom: Mr. and Mrs. Thomas Waldesbuhl's house, Switzerland. Photo: Eric Dutoit, Vevey. (41) Mr. and Mrs. Alfredo de Castro's house, Switzerland. Photo: Eric Dutoit.

Chapter 3. (42) Mr. and Mrs. Cyril Jewsbury's house, England. Photo: Lacy's Studio. (43) Mr. and Mrs. Cyril Jewsbury's house. (44, 45) Mr. and Mrs. Vincent E. Morris's house, Connecticut. (46) Mrs. Merriweather Post's house, Palm Beach, Florida. (47) Top:

Library of Congress, Washington. Bottom: Photo: European. (48) National Trust for Historic Preservation, Washington, D.C. Photo: Marler. (49) Photo: Charles Baptic. (50) Mr. and Mrs. Joseph H. Ziluca's house, Connecticut. Photo: L. Beaugrand. (51) Top left: Photo: Dementi Studio. Top right: Photo: Richmond newspaper, Va. Bottom: Valentine Museum, Va. (52, 53) Mr. and Mrs. Hockstader's house, Connecticut. Photo: Louis Beaugrand.

Chapter 4. (54) Whitney Museum, New York. Photo: Savastano, N.Y. City. (55) Mrs. E. R. Behrend's house. (56) Top: Valentine Museum, Va. Photo; Dementi Studio. Bottom: Australian Consolidated Press.

Chapter 5. (58) from *Chronique d'Angleterre,* by Jean de Wavrin, late 15th century. (61) David Jones Ltd., Sydney. Photo: Australian Consolidated Press. (62) Mrs. Phyllis Landwehr's house, Connecticut. (63) Oneida Silversmiths. (64) Top left: Photo: Richard Averill Smith. Below: Mr. and Mrs. John D. Cowan's house, Connecticut. Photo: Louis Beaugrand. (65) Tiffany & Co. (66, 67) Photo: Richard Averill Smith. (68) Top left: Holmes & Edwards, Inc. Top right: Photo: Richard Averill Smith. Bottom: Holmes & Edwards, Inc. (69) Top and bottom: Photos: Richard Averill Smith. (70) Top: Josiah Wedgwood & Sons Ltd. Center left: Wedgwood. Center right: Photo: Al Hammond. Bottom: Setting arranged by Astrid Sampe for Nordiska Kompaniet, Sweden. Photo: W. Bandhold. (72) Top: The Rijksmuseum, Amsterdam. Bottom: The Cleveland Museum of Art. (73) National Gallery, London. (74) Top: Metropolitan Museum of Art, Dick Fund, 1926. Bottom: Victoria and Albert Museum. (77) Museum of Fine Arts, Boston.

Chapter 6. (78) Photo: Fratelli Alinari. (79) Heraklion Museum, Crete. (80) Right: Metropolitan Museum of Art. Left: E. P. Dutton & Co., Inc., New York. (81) Mr. and Mrs. Rockwell Gardiner's house, Connecticut. Photo: Louis Beaugrand. (85) Mr. and Mrs. Joseph Ziluca's house, Connecticut. Photo: Louis Beaugrand. (87) Mr. and Mrs. Rockwell Gardiner's house. Photo: Louis Beaugrand. (89) Mr. and Mrs. Joseph Ziluca's house. Photo: Louis Beaugrand. (90) Left: Lenox, Inc. Photo: Louis Beaugrand. Right: Lenox, Inc. (91) Left: Brooklyn Museum. Right: Honolulu Academy of Arts. (93) Wedgwood. Photo: Gordon McLeish. (94) Left: The Rosenthal China Corporation. Right: Oxford Bone China. (95) Top: Lenox, Inc. Bottom: Holmes and Edwards, Inc. Photo: Richard Averill Smith. (96, 97) Tables set at David Jones, Inc., Sydney, Australia. (99) The Gorham Co. Table set by Mrs. Robert Hunnicutt, a finalist in the Gorham "Best Dressed Tables" national competition. (100) Mr. and Mrs.

Wayne Hicklin's house, Connecticut. (101) Royal Worcester Porcelain Co.

Chapter 7. (102) Guillaume Egée, 1748-49. Metropolitan Museum of Art. (103) British Museum. (104, 105) Victoria and Albert Museum. (107) Museum of Fine Arts, Boston. (108) Victoria and Albert Museum. (110) Photo: Ed Weddle. (111) Mr. and Mrs. Wayne Hicklin's house, Connecticut. Photo: Louis Beaugrand. (112) Top left and bottom left: Holmes and Edwards, Inc. Right: International Silver Co. (113) Top left and right: Reed & Barton. Bottom left: Oneida Silversmiths. Bottom right: Wedgwood. Photo: Millar & Harris, London. (114) Top: Holmes and Edwards, Inc. Bottom: Georg Jensen, Inc. (115) Top: Photo: Richard Averill Smith. Bottom: Reed & Barton. (117) Mrs. E. R. Behrend's house, Connecticut. (118) Flowers dried and arranged by Mrs. George Hardin Brown. (119) Museo Nazionale, Naples.

Chapter 8. (120) 1875 wood engraving by Speer. Photo: The Bettmann Archive. (121) Baccarat Crystal. Photo: Agneta Fischer. (125) Glass drinking vessels from the collections at Old Sturbridge Village. Photo from *Glass in New England* by Kenneth M. Wilson, and *Old Sturbridge Village* (booklet). (127) Top: Baccarat Crystal. Bottom left: The Newark Museum, Newark, N.J. Bottom right: Baccarat Crystal. (128) Top: Royal Worcester Porcelain Co. Bottom: Tiffany & Co. (129) Steuben Glass. Photo: Herbert Smit. (130) Top: Oneida Silversmiths. Fostoria glassware. Photo: Richard Averill Smith. Center and below: Tiffany & Co. (131) Top and bottom: Baccarat Crystal. (133) Tiffany & Co.

Chapter 9. (134) Vatican Museum, Rome. Photo: Anderson, Rome. (135) Table plan by Juan de la Mata, published in *Arte de Reposteria,* 1747. (136) From *La Science du Maître d'Hôtel* by Monsieur Menon, 1747. (137) Top: Victoria and Albert Museum. Bottom and right: Library of Congress, Washington. (138) From *British Floral Decoration* by R. F. Felton. A. & C. Black Ltd., London, 1910. (139) Collection of Edward G. Robinson. Photo: Peter A. Juley & Son. (140) Left: Museum of Fine Arts, Boston. Right: Dr. Sigmund Ducret, Zürich. (141) Mrs. George Hardin Brown's house, Connecticut. Photo: Louis Beaugrand. (142) Left: Photo: Louis Beaugrand. Right: Photo: Irving Hartley. (143) Wedgwood. (145) Franciscan China, California. Photo: Richard Averill Smith. (146) Georg Jensen, Inc. (147) Mr. and Mrs. Joseph Ziluca's house, Connecticut.

Chapter 10. (148) Mr. and Mrs. Louis Dreyfus's house, New York. (149) Monsieur Chapelain-Midi's house, France. (150) Left and right: Photo: Louis Beaugrand. (151) Top: Mr. Ernest C. Geier's house, Connecticut. Photo: Louis Beaugrand. Bottom: Photo: Louis Beaugrand. (153) The Rosenthal China Corporation. (154) The Gorham Co.

Chapter 11. (156) Photo: Lacy's Studio. (158) Oneida Silversmiths. (159) Oneida Silversmiths. Photo: Richard Averill Smith. (164) Mr. and Mrs. John Delaney's house, Connecticut. (166) Ginori. (167) Photo: Louis Beaugrand.

Chapter 12. (168) Anderson Art Reference Bureau. (170, 171) Museo del Prado, Madrid. (173) Photo: Bibliothèque Nationale, Paris. (174) Painting dated 1626. National Gallery, London. (175) The Louvre. (176) Washington Irving's *Sketchbook.* Published by Dodd Mead, Inc., New York, 1954. (177) "Le Déjeuner." Städelsches Kunstinstitut, Frankfort.

Chapter 13. (178) New York Public Library. Engraving after a design by J. M. Moreau, le Jeune, 1781. (181) The Gorham Co. Table setting by Mrs. Howard J. Grace, a finalist in the Gorham "Best Dressed Tables" national competition. (182) Mr. and Mrs. Walter Hatch's house, Bronxville, N.Y. (185) Tiffany & Co. (186) Ginori. (187) Mr. and Mrs. Alfredo de Castro's house, Switzerland. Photo: Eric Dutoit.

Chapter 14. (188) Victoria and Albert Museum. (189) Musée de Condé. Photo: Giraudon. (190, 191) Photothèque Institut Technique du Vin, Paris. (192) Left: The Walter Hatches, Inc., N.Y. Right: Vevey Museum, Switzerland. (193) Photothèque du Ministère de l'Agriculture. Photo: Pierre Bringé. (194) Left: Photo: Richard Averill Smith. (195) Mr. and Mrs. Thomas Waldesbuhl's house, Switzerland. Photo: Eric Dutoit. (196) Right: Baccarat Crystal. (197) Baccarat Crystal.

Chapter 15. (198) Bayer. Staatsgemäldesammlungen, Munich. (199) Mrs. Anne Valentine Cesare's house. (202) Mr. and Mrs. Cyril Jewsbury's house, England. Photo: Lacy's Studio. (203) Mr. Lester Mac-Kettrick's house, Connecticut. Photo: Louis Beaugrand. (204) Top and bottom: Mr. and Mrs. Cyril Jewsbury's house. Photo: Lacy's Studio. (205) Mr. and Mrs. John Delaney III's house, Connecticut. Photo: Louis Beaugrand. (206) Oneida Silversmiths. Photo: Richard Averill Smith. (207) Mrs. Roger Craig. Photo: Richard Averill Smith.

Chapter 16. (208) New York Public Library (210) Australian Consolidated Press. (211) Mr. and Mrs. Wayne Hicklin's house, Connecticut. Photo: Louis Beaugrand. (212) Top: Rosenthal China Corporation. Bottom: Tiffany & Co. (213) Wedgwood. (214) Top: Tiffany & Co. Bottom: Mr. and Mrs. Walter Hatch's house, Bronxville, N.Y. Photo: Louis Beaugrand. (215) The Gorham Co. (217) Home & Highway Allstate Insurance Co.

Chapter 17. (219) The Gorham Co. (222) Mr. and Mrs. Th. Waldesbuhl's house, Switzerland. Photo: Eric Dutoit. (223) Mr. and Mrs. John J. Delaney's house, Connecticut. Photo: Louis Beaugrand. (225) Mr. and Mrs. Louis Dreyfus's house, New York. Photo: Louis Beaugrand. (227) Below: Mr. Ernest C. Geier's house, Connecticut.

Chapter 18. (228) Mr. and Mrs. Joseph Ziluca's house, Connecticut. (229) Courtesy of Mr. and Mrs. Walter Hatch. Photo: Louis Beaugrand. (232) Top: Mr. and Mrs. Hockstader's house, Connecticut. Photo: Louis Beaugrand. Bottom: Consulate General of Japan, N.Y. (233) Consulate General of Japan, N.Y (234, 235) Victoria and Albert Museum. (236) Mr. and Mrs. Cyril Jewsbury's house, England. Photo: Lacy's Studio. (238) Victoria and Albert Museum. (239) Colonial Williamsburg. (240) The Tea Council, N.Y. (241) Photo: Richard Averill Smith. (243) From Grandville's *Les Fleurs Animées,* translated by N. Cleaveland. R. Martin, New York, 1849.

Chapter 19. (244) Photo: Louis Beaugrand. (247) Photo: Louis Beaugrand. (248) Hallmark Cards. (249) American Swedish News Exchange. (250, 251) Courtesy of Mr. and Mrs. Rockwell Gardiner, Connecticut. Photos: Louis Beaugrand. (252) Top and bottom: The Tea Council of the U.S.A., N.Y.

Chapter 20. (254) The Gorham Co. Table setting by Mrs. Boswell Johnson, a member of the Ikebana Garden Club, Memphis, and a finalist in the Gorham "Best Dressed Tables" national competition. (255) Philadelphia Museum of Art. (258) The Gorham Co. (259) Mrs. E. R. Behrend's house, Connecticut.

Chapter 21. (260) Mrs. Anne Valentine Cesare's house. (261) Teina Baumstone. (263, 265) New York Public Library.

The majority of the contemporary table settings that appear in this book were created by the author.